Jenny —
Enjoy!
Always remember —
It's all for Jesus!
Victoria

THROUGH CRACKED GLASS

Jenn,

Enjoy!

Always remember...

It's all for Jesus!

Michele

Through Cracked Glass

Grace for God's fractured and imperfect children

Victoria Rose

XULON PRESS

Xulon Press
2301 Lucien Way #415
Maitland, FL 32751
407.339.4217
www.xulonpress.com

© 2019 by Victoria Rose

All rights reserved solely by the author. The author guarantees all contents are original and do not infringe upon the legal rights of any other person or work. No part of this book may be reproduced in any form without the permission of the author. The views expressed in this book are not necessarily those of the publisher.

Unless otherwise indicated, Scripture quotations taken from the Holy Bible, New International Version (NIV). Copyright © 1973, 1978, 1984, 2011 by Biblica, Inc.™. Used by permission. All rights reserved.

Illustrated by Gwenn Copeland-Davenport:
fragmented.art.studios@gmail.com

Printed in the United States of America.

ISBN-13: 978-1-54567-921-0

Table of Contents

Foreword. vii

Preface – It All Began at Home xiii

Section I - Perseverance

Opening – The Hiding Place 3
Introduction – Keep on Keeping On 5
Chapter 1: My Desert Place of
 Beginning 11
Chapter 2: Come Away and Rest. 18
Chapter 3: Lessons in a Cemetery. 27
Chapter 4: The Squeaky Snow and
 a Boat 36
Chapter 5: Life is Hard and Other
 Truths. 44
Chapter 6: Sunrise Over the Water 53
Chapter 7: My Someday Country 60
Chapter 8: Wrestling. 68
Chapter 9: A Lesson from Habakkuk . . . 77

Section II – Forgiveness

Opening – Jess and the Sparrow. 83
Introduction – Forgiveness –
 Why is It So Difficult? . . . 89
Chapter 1: Forgiving Ourselves. 93
Chapter 2: Divorce One 101

Chapter 3: When Forgiveness Hurts
            Too Much 109
Chapter 4: The Hike 120
Chapter 5: Jonah's Legacy 128
Chapter 6: Jaw-Cracking and
            Peace-Making 137

Section III – Serving

Opening – Wings................. 149
Introduction – Helping, Serving,
               Healing 153
Chapter 1: Momma................ 161
Chapter 2: Dad.................. 165
Chapter 3: Billy Bob 171
Chapter 4: Finding Our Way
            Back Home 178
Chapter 5: A Little Lamb.......... 184
Chapter 6: When Our Hearts
            Fall Down 190
Chapter 7: Coming Alongside 198
Chapter 8: The Unworthy Ones....... 202
Chapter 9: Let Me Help You 213
Chapter 10: Story People 223

Epilogue 229

About the Author 235

Foreword

When was the last time you examined your life? Before you answer, I don't mean a toe in the pool of subconsciousness; rather a high dive into its darkest depths. Did you analyze your thoughts and emotions in such a way that a defined narrative could emerge? If so, would you be brave enough to share that private world with its public counterpart?

The book you're about to read is the cumulative knowledge of a life still unfolding. It is a study in self-reflection, discovery, learning, and salvation. It is a glimpse into the psyche of a little girl growing up in rural Michigan, trying to figure out life from parents still trying to figure out their own lives, and the woman she becomes from lessons, both taught and learned, along the way.

For reasons other than biological, I call that woman Mom, and I consider myself fortunate to be a minor cast member in her story.

I met Victoria's son around six years ago. We were the same age; our daughters were the same age. The trajectories of our lives were similar. We shared similar tastes in music and movies... and we were both in prison, far from home, for causing a death by drinking and driving.

It's human nature to seek out people you relate to. This simple, social practice becomes near impossible in prison when you're a career-oriented family man with no criminal history. I was lucky to become fast friends with Jeremy and, soon enough, his family.

A prison's visitation park presents an interesting dichotomy. For the inmate, it's a haven; a chance to escape his new reality and spend some time with loved ones. For the visitors, it's a glimpse behind the curtain of a completely different society; one they never considered as a possibility for their loved ones.

Despite the draconian surroundings, there's always an easy familiarity and fellowship. It reminds me of arrivals and departures at the airport the way families and loved ones greet one another; some laughing, some crying. Most are nervous, while for some, it's just a walk in the park. Oftentimes, people say, "I'll see you soon"; sometimes people just say goodbye.

That's where I met Jeremy's wonderful family. They came every weekend to visit him, and I was the inmate assigned to run the "canteen." Because we weren't usually busy (it was a small work camp), I was often invited to join their conversations and occasionally have lunch with them.

At some point, Victoria decided she was adopting me, and I became a member of the family. As a thirty- something, adoption had never seemed like a viable option, but I wasn't complaining.

I'm no longer at the same institution as Jeremy; however, Victoria has been a constant pen pal for over four years now. In that time, I've come to admire and respect everything about her. She constantly amazes me with her unshakeable faith, her altruism and integrity, her drive to do what's right, and the empathy on display with each random act of kindness.

This is a woman who walked away from her life and career to take care of her parents when they needed her. A woman who abandoned everything she knew and moved 1,100 miles across the country when her son needed her. A woman who sponsors children across the globe through a nonprofit, Christian organization. A woman who uses journalism as a tool to better her community through not only reporting on an issue, but calling every reader to action. This is a woman that opens her door for friends and her heart for the world.

Some stories need to be told and others need to be heard. This book represents both. Victoria once told me, "When we allow God to use us, even though our imperfections show, the beautiful colors show even more. Isn't it a comfort to know our Heavenly Father uses us, His fractured and imperfect children, to spread the good news to other fractured and imperfect people?"

I've been blessed with Victoria's guidance, encouragement, and, most of all, friendship. She saw in me a fractured and imperfect soul, and she smiled. With this story, she smiles on each of us.

Enjoy!

— Storm Wood

Preface

IT ALL BEGAN AT HOME

I was raised in a conservative home, with hard-working and resourceful parents. I didn't know what I was missing until many years later, after I was grown and with a family of my own, when I struggled so much more than I thought I should have to. I never felt like I was doing enough or loving enough. My mom had a way of making you feel inadequate. She used this phrase often – "I'll do it myself!" — which was her way of saying she didn't approve of how I did it – whatever "it" was. It could be washing dishes or making a bed or folding towels. She wasn't good at building up your self-esteem, but excelled in tearing it down, although I don't believe she understood the damage she was doing to my sensitive psyche all those years.

For my mom and dad, it was a long way from the mountains of West Virginia where they were born and raised. They both grew up poor, Mom's family more so than Dad's, so frugality reigned in our blue-collar household. My parents, shortly after they were married, moved to Michigan to find work and build a life together. Dad's dad made him promise not to get a job in the coal mines; he wanted a safer life for his son. My Papaw had been injured in the mines, retiring early from his disability. I remember he walked with a limp, his cane never far from his hand. He was the son of a Native American woman, married to a white man, and his strong, square jaw and high cheekbones told of his rock-solid heritage.

Dad, who didn't graduate high school and dropped out in his junior year because of a disagreement with the teacher, worked hard at his new job in the shop for General Motors. He worked even harder improving his chances for advancement by not only receiving his GED, but taking classes at night to become an electrician, working many long hours at the shop for over thirty years and then retiring in his early fifties.

In Dad's lifetime, he's built three houses, remodeled many more, bought and sold real estate on a small scale, and, coupled with his conservative frugality, has always had enough to provide for his family to comfortably live on.

Life, I've always believed, is full of lessons. Some lessons are expressly taught to us by our parents, while some are taught by observation; and others are learned by watching the things we don't want to repeat in our own lives.

I can still hear Mom reminding me to brush my teeth and make my bed, pick up my clothes and finish my homework. I can hear Dad encouraging me to think things through and get good grades. My favorite Dad phrase is: "You can do anything you put your mind to." I watched them both and learned about the importance of hard work and living within my means. I learned about honesty and faithfulness. And I learned, from watching Momma hang on to anger for years, how necessary it was to let go of hurts and cultivate a forgiving spirit. I learned, from watching Dad, to be more adventuresome and not to be afraid of stepping far outside my comfort zone to reach my goal.

That's not to say the lessons I learned I learned perfectly and always follow them, because I've had to relearn some pretty basic lessons more than once.

Mom's been gone now for a little over three years, and Dad's reaching his stride. The house was Momma's domain, and her personality, for such a small person, filled the house so that her moods and wants dictated what happened there. What was on TV had to have her approval, and every conversation, whether face to face or on the phone, was open to her prying and prodding questions. She needed to know everything about everything, whether it concerned her directly or not.

As an adolescent, I perfected the art of deflecting her questions and avoiding conversations altogether because I knew how they'd end. Her constant prying coupled with her inability to fully understand what I was saying was exhausting, so I did what I did best and retreated into my fantasy world of books, where I'd read one after another after another until I was sated. The school library was my best friend, where I checked out as many books as they'd allow and I could carry, balancing as many as fifteen precariously in my arms as I walked the quarter mile home from the bus stop. I anticipated the wonderful lands and experiences I'd have far away from my mom's questions, my brother's annoying behavior, and my sister's current neuroses.

Now that Momma's gone, Dad can finally just be himself. He can watch what he wants, buy the food he wants, go where and when he wants. After the initial grief-and-adjustment period, he has rallied and, for the first time in his life, has no one who is second-guessing his motives. That's pretty liberating, I would think.

He's even learning how to play piano. With his early Parkinson's, forcing his fingers to play the correct notes has been great physical therapy. I have a gorgeous, mahogany grand piano I had to leave at my parents' house because it was too expensive to ship it to where I live, plus I don't really have the space right now. So, I'm glad it's getting some use.

Not to speak ill of the dead, as the saying goes, because I loved my Momma, and she had some truly commendable qualities. But I also know what it was like growing up under her thumb and microscope. She was a product of her own upbringing back in the mountains of West Virginia, where life was exhausting and crying was a luxury you couldn't afford. She became a mother just shy of her seventeenth birthday, with three small children by the time she was twenty. Dad worked long hours, so it was up to her to keep her babies fed, clean, and safe, and the house clean too. She did her best; I'm convinced of it.

Her own mother died of complications from breast cancer eight short days before my sister was born. I can't imagine the depth of her grief at not being able to attend her mom's funeral, and shortly thereafter holding her firstborn child, knowing they'd never meet. I know not having her mom to go to for advice and encouragement hurt her deeply. She had no family in Michigan, and no friends to speak of, so she did what she had to do to get through each day.

Understanding that now helps, but back then, I didn't understand how her own family life had shaped her into who she became. She was the youngest of seven children, with five brothers between her and her sister, the firstborn. To say she was spoiled is putting it mildly. I came to the realization one day that I was raised in a home where my mom's love was conditional. Either you towed the line, or you got the brunt of her temper. Of course I didn't understand that then because, well, that's all I knew. I have no memories of hugs as a child. I grew up not knowing what it felt like to be embraced by a loving mother and to have my tears wiped away. "What are you crying for?" was a phrase I didn't like to hear. If I wanted any attention, I had to work for it, and I usually didn't try. I wish I could have understood to what extent that upbringing would affect the lives of my own children, as I raised them using the only experience I had to draw from. I only hope, over time, they will forgive me where I failed them.

My older sister, and the firstborn, was mentally handicapped, a diagnosed schizophrenic with constant issues and needs, so the bulk of attention went to her. My older brother, like a dark-haired Dennis the Menace™, was by far Mom's favorite. Then when my youngest brother was born three months premature, after Mom's two miscarriages, well, her love was now laser-focused on him, which is understandable. I had been the baby of the family for fourteen years and now faded into the background even more. I didn't ask for things and I didn't make waves; it was safer that way.

As an adult, God began to show me the deficits in my character that needed work.

The big one was learning about unconditional love. What did that mean exactly? How was it accomplished? The first thing God taught me was to stop pulling back when I got hurt, because building emotional walls was my specialty. This idea was very hard for me because I had perfected the art of pulling back and retreating to my safe place many years before. Certain words or looks would trigger this survival instinct and the wall would go up before I even realized what was happening. Once it was there, I didn't know how to break it down, because the wall didn't just keep others away; it trapped me in a prison of my own making.

Vulnerability was an anathema to me. Protecting myself from pain was my priority, and boy, did I know how to do it. On my first blog from years ago, started for cathartic reasons, I posted the following:

> *It began many years ago, while still married to my first husband. As I matured and our marriage deteriorated, feelings of being insecure – and by that, I mean my husband didn't have my back – grew. I had to decide.*
>
> *Collapse or stand.*
>
> *I chose to stand. Alone.*

After all, there were others depending on me. I couldn't let them down.

My second marriage wasn't any better. Same song and dance.

It became a way of life. A habit. It is what defined me.

So, I've been known to all my friends and family as a strong, independent and free-spirited woman for many years.

And I'm really tired. So very tired.

How many times had I emotionally retreated, back behind a barrier I'd built to protect me from pain? For years, I thought protecting myself was the way to survive. But all it did was make me fearful and small-hearted. I missed out on so much.

One day, God showed me He wanted something better for me. Being vulnerable was necessary for my growth. And in loving unconditionally, He told me, "You will be completely vulnerable, and you will be hurt, badly."

"But it will be worth it."

I read somewhere once that when children are grown, they may, one day, forgive their parents. We reach a point in our own growth where we see their flaws and begin to understand our own. That's what we humans are, full of flaws. We love each other anyway, though, because love is a powerful leveler.

As the apostle Peter says in I Peter 4:8, *"Above all, love each other deeply, because love covers over a multitude of sins."*

The short stories in this book are snapshots of lessons God has shown me over the years, and I hope they'll be encouraging to you.

He loves us in our messes and works with us to make us more and more like Jesus.

Persevere and enjoy the journey.

Section One

PERSEVERANCE

The Hiding Place

My heart retreats again;
Back into its deep recesses
Where safety seems sure;
Where the pain you inflict cannot reach.
All is still.

Paralyzed, I cannot feel love.
I cannot grasp the need to forgive
Once more,
Why do you keep hurting me?
Do I deserve this?

And why must I forgive again
And again
And again?
I am weary and beaten.
Oblivion beckons.

Oh, Beloved Shepherd,
Remove the barrier around my heart.

Your hands are healing hands.
Your touch is solace.
Your words bring peace.

The still waters soothe.
The green pastures sustain.
Your presence protects.
Rest my soul; You are safe here.
Restoration arrives.

Keep on Keeping On – Perseverance in The Journey

Every one of us, without exception, comes from places of deep brokenness, and God delights in transforming us into beautiful jewels.

The following, short chapters are about important truths God showed me over a period of years when I had been wandering in a wilderness of disappointment and discouragement for most of my adult life. I had two failed marriages to my name and, being a Christian, divorce had never been an option before. My life fell apart not once, but twice. A lot of re-thinking happened during that time, and a lot of healing.

The task was to overcome something severely hindering me in my spiritual growth; something I didn't even know was there until

God revealed it one day, when I had been an adult doing adult things for many years.

Satan, that accuser of the brethren, had convinced me from childhood that I was not enough. I wasn't good enough. I didn't do enough. I had too many character flaws. I was too prickly and too aloof. I was pushy and opinionated. I can still hear my mom saying to me when I was a child, "Left-handed people can't do nothing right." Those words still hurt.

My first husband, from his innate need for complete control, made sure I understood I was nothing on my own, and that everything I had was only because of him. He took every opportunity to make me feel worthless and unworthy of being loved. Years of this constant verbal and emotional beat-down took its toll.

My second husband told me I was prickly and cold. He wanted me to be a different person than who I was. When he said he hated me, I believed I was somehow deficient and undeserving of anyone's love. My mistakes were too big, and I became a disappointment to not just my friends and family but myself as well.

I was not enough. I had never been enough. Enter, God.

It happened during my second divorce. God providentially ensconced me in Arizona where I lived all alone for four years. He used the mountains and the desert to heal a broken heart that was bleeding out. I was a Michigander by birth and was happy to leave not just the cold weather, gray skies, and mosquitos, but the level of stress that was killing me.

That God-imposed isolation was crucial to my growth and healing. My heavenly Father took the time to gently teach me something so powerful, it upended everything I had believed about myself up to that point in time. I was His special treasure, cherished, and beloved. No one had ever made me feel that way before. It was a brand-new experience and I soaked it up. Those years in Arizona hiking in the desert and mountains, communing with God, changed my life. My heart is still there.

This is what I learned: I am enough. I have always been enough.

After four years, God sent me back to Michigan to live in my parents' basement and help my dad care for my mom after she was diagnosed with dementia, where a whole host of new lessons were learned.

Then God spirited me away to Florida, where the lessons have continued.

As you read these snippets about perseverance and endurance, I hope they'll be as encouraging to you as learning the lessons were to me.

They aren't all chronological, and I've had to re-learn some lessons over and over, so don't feel discouraged when it happens to you.

One of the wonderful things about our heavenly Father is that He's patient with us, like a shepherd with his sheep.

"My sheep listen to my voice; and I know them, and they follow me." (John 10:27)

I absolutely love how Brennan Manning, in his book *The Furious Longing of God,* describes the depth of our Father's love: "The foundation of the furious longing of God is the Father who is the originating Lover, the Son who is the full self-expression of that Love, and the Spirit who is the original and inexhaustible activity of that Love, drawing the created universe into himself." (2009).

He carefully watches over us and searches for us when we wander off, lovingly bringing us back to the flock. He doesn't abandon us to our fate – He comes and finds us, rescuing us from the consequences of our own actions. He gently binds up our wounds.

He leads us by still waters and brings us to green meadows, where He restores our souls.

That's the kind of God worth living for.

Chapter 1

My Desert Place of Beginning

It might be hard to believe, but I love cactus plants. Do you want to know why? They absorb the most intense heat from the burning sun and smothering, breathless air and grow anyway. They seem almost defiant in their ability to use their environment to their best advantage.

When I lived in Arizona, I had a prickly pear cactus a friend gave me, growing in a pot on my patio. It was thriving and becoming top heavy, since it was outgrowing its container. One morning, I woke up to find during the night it had toppled off the stand I had it sitting on and some of the pads had broken off, leaving it tattered. I carefully picked it up and placed it back on the stand. I sadly looked it over with chagrin, feeling bad that some of its newest growth was gone. It looked beaten up and I hoped it was going to be alright.

Not more than two weeks later, I noticed several little nubs right next to where the pads had been broken off. New growth, in the scorching heat of an Arizona summer.

God, the author of life, can make us grow no matter where we are or how damaged we've become.

"You, God, are my God, earnestly I seek you; I thirst for you, my whole being longs for you, in a dry and parched land where there is no water." (Psalm 63:1)

I love what C.H. Spurgeon, that great preacher of grace, said about King David's Psalm 63:

> This was probably written while David was fleeing from Absalom... and hard pressed by those who sought his life. David did not leave off singing because he was in the wilderness, neither did he in slovenly idleness go on repeating Psalms intended for

other occasions; but he carefully made his worship suitable to his circumstances, and presented to his God a wilderness hymn when he was in the wilderness. There was no desert in his heart, though there was a desert around him. We too may expect to be cast into rough places ere we go hence. In such seasons, may the Eternal Comforter abide with us, and cause us to bless the Lord at all times, making even the solitary place to become a temple for Jehovah. (Psalm 63 by C. H. Spurgeon)

Arizona is in the Sonoran Desert, and, to me, this one-of-a-kind desert is a fascinating place. Nowhere else in the world will you find the stately saguaro cactus; they're unique to the Sonoran Desert. They're slow-growing and reach as much as sixty feet or more in height and can live to a ripe old age of 200 years. Their root system is shallow – only about four to six inches deep— with laterally growing roots reaching out as far as they are tall, ready to drink up every drop of water that falls within their grasp.

You'd never use the word "lush" for the Sonoran Desert. It doesn't have bright gardens or thick woods like the Midwest, but neither is it barren. This desert is prickly and not overly inviting, at least at first. And yet I love to walk through it absorbing its history and examining the wide variety of plants and the type of critters scurrying around.

There are lizards of all sizes, scorpions, tarantulas, javelina, coyote, and the occasional mountain lion. But mostly, you see the scrub plants, small palo verde, and mesquite trees growing, providing a smattering of shade, waving their branches to their Creator at the bluest of blue skies and the undulating waves of heat, for that's what they were made to thrive in.

If you observe the desert carefully, you'll find flowering plants growing right out of rock. How do they do that, I wonder? How did that seed find enough shelter to sprout, and something for its roots to grab on to? You can almost see God stooping low to carefully place that seed right in the shade of the crack between two unmoving stones. "There you go! A perfect spot," I can almost hear Him say. And the seed gives thanks for its safe and dark home, only able to sprout and grow, producing beautiful flowers because of His granting.

You'll find blooms of yellows, pinks, oranges, and whites perched atop prickly pear, saguaro, ocotillo, cholla, and other cacti, brightening the landscape like a welcome drink for thirsty eyes. After a good rain, the palo verde trees, with their green trunks, push out tiny teardrop leaves, producing cheerful golden yellow blooms. I think it's their way of giving thanks for the water of life.

These resilient plants of the Sonoran Desert wait in a spirit of anticipation and thankfulness for the water they receive from the One who created them. They use what they need and store the rest for those times of drought they know all too well.

The rocks, so huge some of them, appear ancient. I always wonder just how long they've been there and what they've seen. Were they pushed up out of the ground centuries ago? What was it like to be born that way? They seem to have stories to tell, like old men waiting for you to pull up a chair and ask them what's up. Sometimes I stand next to one of these behemoths, gently place my hand on its sun-warm surface, and whisper, with my face close to it, "How old are you? What have you seen?"

Such mysteries! The way the setting sun haloes the spines of a towering saguaro at twilight is a wonderful sight. To come around a bend in the rocky path and discover a long-dead, toppled cactus – its sun-bleached skeleton lying there so quietly makes you feel as if you're in a beloved graveyard, filled with the spirits of cactus sentinels of old, keeping watch over the living.

And then, to drink in the glory and beauty of the slowly setting sun, the colors in that most intensely beautiful of endless blue skies, changing to pinks and oranges and then fading ever so slowly to dusky blue, and then darker and darker until the mountains disappear as if they'd never been there, makes it seem as if you're in a magical land where anything can happen.

Before Arizona, I had always pictured deserts as unwelcoming places. But since living there, I see them in a whole new light.

God has His people where He needs them. He can make us do more than survive but thrive, when we're in the right places. Just as Paul said in Philippians 4:12, *"I know what it is to be in need, and I know what it is to have plenty. I have learned the secret of being content in any and every situation, whether well fed or hungry, whether living in plenty or in want."*

God's grace is wherever His people are. Keep your eyes open to the wonderful mysteries He has for you individually. Each journey is unique, important, and part of His plan.

Chapter 2

COME AWAY AND REST

I would have to say that for much of my time in Arizona, my heart was at peace and calm, and I was pretty much stress-free. Unrushed. God's lessons were interspersed with periods of rest, where I knew myself to be tenderly watched over, protected, and provided for.

I had arrived there with a heart crushed by worry and anxiety. It took me a few days to stop shaking every time my phone would ring, anticipating more unpleasant news. A failing marriage and a financial crisis consumed my every waking moment. I couldn't figure out how to fix all the problems, and the high level of stress made it difficult to think clearly. The peace and quiet and solitude of my new home began to calm my spirit and ready me for what was to come.

I can recall several stories of specific grace where God showered me with unexpected kindness, just to show me how much He loved me.

We're all familiar with the Lord's Prayer, right? Here's what Brennan Manning said about it in *The Furious Longing of God*.

> *Our Father.* Familiar words, maybe so familiar that they are no longer real. Those words were not only real, but also revolutionary to the twelve disciples. Pagan philosophers such as Aristotle arrived at the existence of God via human reason and referred to Him in vague, impersonal terms: *the uncaused cause, the immovable mover.* The prophets of Israel revealed the God of Abraham, Isaac, and Jacob in a warmer, more compassionate manner. But only Jesus revealed to an astonished Jewish community that God

> is truly Father. If you took the love of all the best mothers and fathers who have lived in the course of human history, all their goodness, kindness, patience, fidelity, wisdom, tenderness, strength, and love and united all those qualities in a single person, that person's love would only be a faint shadow of the furious love and mercy in the heart of God the Father addressed to you and me at this moment. (2009)

That's the Father who tenderly took care of me every day.

I arrived in Arizona without a job, and after seven weeks of sending out resumes and being interviewed, I obtained employment through a temp agency, so I was on probation for ninety days. It was imperative I make a good impression so the company would want to hire me directly at the end of my probationary period.

I had my morning routine. Because I have OCD tendencies, I always put my keys in the same place - on the side table near the front door, because then I would know where they were. All you other OCD readers will understand.

And, getting ready to walk out the door for work, I had four things I always, always, always had with me – and in a specific hand. Like I said – routine.

On my right shoulder was my purse. In my right hand was the handle of my rolling bag. In my left hand was my cup of coffee and my keys (well, the key ring was on my finger). This was etched in stone. I never wavered or walked out the door until I had these four things.

That morning, I did everything the same. Or, so I thought.

I checked to make sure the windows were locked. I checked to make sure the sliding glass door was locked. I walked out the front door and it locked behind me.

Suddenly I experienced that awful, sinking feeling. You know the one I mean. I looked at my left hand and discovered I didn't have my keys.

I looked in the window of the sliding glass door and saw them right where I always placed them – on the small table.

Unreachable.

Of course, I instinctively turned the front doorknob. Locked. I tried the sliding glass door. Locked. I looked at the windows. Locked. I tried the doors again. Still locked.

What to do? "Ok, God," I said. "I need some help here, please." I couldn't afford to be late for work. I was still a new employee and working on making a good impression with my supervisor.

I stood there, looking at my locked front door, my brain spinning around like a hamster on a wheel. No solution came to mind.

A voice whispered in my ear – "Try the sliding glass door again."

"But I've already tried it twice! It's locked!"

"Try it anyway."

So, I did. And it opened, quite easily. I stood there on the threshold, rooted in place, uncomprehendingly looking at the keys across the room on the table when the voice spoke again – "Now, Victoria, we can't be late for work. Go get your keys."

Yes, this really happened.

As my faith grew and my reliance on my heavenly Father increased, Jesus and I had many conversations about anything and everything. He was as real to me as if He were physically standing next to me. There were many times I felt I could just about see Him. I know many Christians believe they should pray more, but we sadly miss the point. It's not 'prayer' like you'd normally think of it. It's talking, chatting; having a conversation with someone you love, and who loves you. It's that sharing thing you do with friends, family, and spouses.

It's so easy. It's not mysterious or hard at all. It's just communicating.

I remember one day when God and I were discussing my finances. "You know," I said, "if I could just earn more than I do now, I'd be able to pay my bills more easily." A couple of months later, I got transferred to the sales department at work where I not only received an increase in my base pay, but started earning bonuses. And guess what? You got it – my income doubled! Really. I'm not making this up.

Then there was the time when I was given – yes given – a beautiful spinning wheel by a truly kind-hearted lady. I guess I should elaborate just a bit. About twenty years before, I had fallen in love with handweaving and spinning and had taught myself how to do both. I had a weaving loom and hand-painted spinning wheel back in Michigan. After a few months in Arizona, my creative juices had started flowing again and I wanted to get back into the craft.

I found a spinning wheel on Craigslist for $250. I thought I could just about handle spending that amount of money, so I called the seller who brought it over for me to look at. We discovered there was a small piece missing, so the seller said she'd take the wheel, get it repaired, and then call me back and I could let her know then if I still wanted to purchase it. A couple of weeks went by. When she called, she said, "You know, I was telling my daughter about you, and I decided I don't want to sell the wheel – I want to give it to you." Really; I'm not making this up either.

The things we think are just too small for our heavenly Father to care about are the things He does care about. He is our Father and delights in taking care of us. We should let Him do it more often. It's a win/win situation.

> *Therefore, I tell you, do not worry about your life, what you will eat or drink; or about your body, what you will wear. Is not life more than food, and the body more than clothes? Look at the birds of the air; they do not sow or reap or store away in barns, and yet your heavenly Father feeds them. Are you not much more valuable than they? (Matthew 6:25-26)*

We convince ourselves we're not that important, or that we can do it on our own, and we end up missing out on so much our Father wants to do for us.

This is not to say, of course, that He gives us everything we want. I could write another chapter about times when He's said 'no' to my earnest prayers.

Remember how Jesus, in Matthew 19:14, said we need to come to Him as little children? How many times have you said no to your toddler when she wanted a cookie because you knew it would spoil her dinner? But then again, how many times have you showered your sweet-faced, sparkly-eyed love of your life with kisses and snuggles and toys and special treats, only because of your great love for her?

This is the same way our Father treats us, His beloved children. He showers us with light, love, and laughter, and so much more that brings us joy, that when He says 'no' shouldn't overshadow what we experience as His love for us.

He wants our trust to be complete. As a small child sleeps securely in her father's lap, totally unafraid, so God wants us to rest securely in His love as well.

Chapter 3

Lessons in a Cemetery

We took the long way around instead of the shortcut. I thought we were headed to the shopping center, but, once we got near, Mom said, "No, we need to turn right on the road up ahead."

"Really," I said, "are you sure? I thought the store was in the same place where you grocery shop."

"No," she said, "It's in front of that big store – you know – whatchacallit."

"Ummm..." I cast around in my memory bank, "do you mean Meijer?"

"Yes," she said with her infectious smile, "that's the one!" Ah, ok, then.

We found the store.

I almost lost Mom in the store though.

We split up after a little while, and then I couldn't find her. My heart started to beat faster and I felt a slight panic building in the general area of my gut. I pictured myself calling Dad and saying, "Dear God, I've lost Mom!"

But I finally found her calmly working her way down another aisle.

We finished in that store and decided to kill some time in Meijer, so we did, and I stayed close this time, not letting her out of my sight.

Later that evening, we went for a walk together, my mom and me. Enjoying the fall colors, we strolled around the corner, past the Methodist church, and stopped outside the village cemetery, where we lingered for a few minutes and chatted. Michigan is well-known for its beautiful fall foliage. Tree-lined streets covered with golden and orange leaves glowing in the sunlight give the village a transient beauty it doesn't truly possess.

She asked me if I'd ever been in that cemetery to read any of the headstones, but I told her I hadn't yet. It was small, with some old headstones, and some newer ones as well. I wasn't in the mood to be so somber this evening after the taxing day I'd had.

But the scene was quaint in the extreme – an old, whitewashed church with a cemetery right next to it. Headstones with names of husbands and wives and children, their days and names etched in stone as their memories are etched in hearts.

A place of hope, overlooking a place of sadness, to remind us to hope.

Singing hymns of worship and praise on Sundays to strengthen hearts weighed down with sorrow.

The living and the dead close together. Why do we remove ourselves now so far from our pain? We avoid pain because it hurts so, and who wants to hurt?

I believe, though, that when we embrace our pain, it loses its power to destroy us. Instead, it allows us to take comfort in our memories and begin to heal.

With my mom's dementia, she lost bits and pieces of her memory on an almost daily basis. I needed to embrace this pain of loss so my memories in the years to come would bring me comfort instead of shame, because each day caring for her became more and more difficult.

During her slow decline, I occasionally wrote about what she was up to. Sharing this journey with others was beneficial to not just myself, but for my friends who read about our struggles.

One of mom's new "things" is cutting the towels and sheets up into smaller pieces to wrap around her dolls for blankets – she thinks they're alive. She uses safety pins. I had to temporarily take the scissors away from her the other week because she was carrying them around in her pocket. I told her she couldn't do that. She gave me her sour face. But I smiled and said I was only telling her the same things I would tell my kids when they were growing up.

She likes to try and feed her dolls food. She puts it in their mouths and then takes a butter knife and scrapes it back out, all the while chattering at them. She kisses them and holds them and sleeps with them. She doesn't like to leave them and gets agitated if she forgets where she puts one. She sits in her rocking chair and hums softly to them and smiles and laughs.

She's like a little girl playing tea party. But the tea party never ends and Momma's not playing.

This past summer, I caught her using furniture polish outside on the porch, thinking it was bug spray. And another day we found her using toilet bowl cleaner to wash the vinyl floor. And another day she was ironing the carpet.

She found a small bud vase with a large enough opening, so she fills it with ice and then places it in the refrigerator. I don't know why. Neither does she.

At dinner, if she has both a fork and a spoon, she gets confused about which one to use. If she starts using the fork, then she can't use the spoon, and vice versa. She'll sit there with her hands in her lap, looking at the food on her plate. It's as if she's attempting to summon instructions as to what she's supposed to do next.

She doesn't understand most conversations anymore. I can say to her – the sun is nice and bright today! – and she'll respond with something completely off topic. I keep our conversations, such as they are, as simple and direct as possible.

She asks for my permission to do things: to eat something; to wash something in the washing machine. I've become her momma.

She won't remember what she had for dinner, but she will remember something she did months before.

Dad is three different people in her mind. He's a woman, for some reason, in the mornings when he makes her breakfast. Then he's either a good guy or a mean guy, depending on what mood she's in and what color shirt he's wearing. If she gets mad at him, and he changes his shirt, she'll sit down next to him and tell him about the "mean" guy. She doesn't remember who Dad is – that they've known each other since they were teenagers and they've been married for almost sixty years.

But she remembers that I'm her daughter, at least for now. And she remembers her other three children, and some of her grandchildren and great-grandchildren. She can tell us about things that happened years ago with good clarity, and then not be able to put together a name with the face.

It's like there are missing puzzle pieces in her brain. Arbitrary empty spaces where bits of information are gone. How can you completely forget who a person is, but remember scenes in which he was there?

She looks at pictures of Dad that were taken recently, but when she looks at him in the flesh, they don't look the same to her. I've held a photograph of him right up next to his face and she doesn't think they're the same person. How does the brain short-circuit like that?

What she sees and what she hears doesn't get translated correctly somehow.

She wanders from room to room, looking for things to do, I guess. She always loved to clean, so I think that's what she's doing, looking for something that needs cleaning. So, she's constantly rearranging furniture and pictures and knick-knacks.

And when she can't find something, she tries to accuse us of making off with it, which, of course, isn't true. Dad goes hunting around until he locates whatever she's squirreled away in some strange place that you wouldn't normally expect to find whatever it is you're looking for.

Dementia is a cruel thief, stealing more than memories. It's like a fog that grows thicker and thicker, eventually obliterating everything, leaving only blankness and isolation. The ones you loved the most are strangers to you, as if your knowledge of them had never been. Your world shrinks ever smaller until it completely disappears.

All diseases are tragic, but dementia does more than destroy the body. It reduces the family to children crying in anguish, because of the betrayal of a parent who should have always loved them. A mother who wasn't supposed to be able to forget who they were.

Watching Momma's dementia empty her brain of every comfort-giving memory, I've learned to confront my pain. We can try to run from what tortures us, but it follows us wherever we go because it's inside our hearts.

I've stopped running from myself and now take the time to visit those graves of

LESSONS IN A CEMETERY

disappointment and hurt. When I hand it all over to God in worship, I feel the wounds that have been festering begin to heal.

The pain decreases, and the scars left behind are testimonies to the lessons learned and the fires survived.

Our pain makes us stronger and more resilient – becoming the help to others they so desperately need.

Chapter 4

The Squeaky Snow and a Boat

When our circumstances get the best of us, we may sink into a deep depression. Some personalities are more prone to depression than others, and for those who don't experience it, it can be difficult for them to understand what's happening to their loved ones. When I'm depressed, I draw back like a tortoise into its shell. I become isolated and fatigue dogs my steps. I have no desire to be with anyone or do anything. My waking moments are consumed with my situation and darkness seems to hover over my days.

Not too many months after my son was convicted, sentenced, and imprisoned for eleven years, I hit rock-bottom and it took many weeks to finally feel the light of the sun on my face again. I couldn't hear God over the noise

The Squeaky Snow and a Boat

of my internal screaming, and the hard-won lessons of Arizona dissipated like fog.

He let me traverse this dark valley, and once I reached the other side, I was a different person. For those who desire to understand what a depressive episode is, I've described it here for you.

While I was in that cycle of deep disappointment and hurt, I wrote the following and posted it on the blog I had started for my son.

The squeaky snow, now drifted across the sidewalk, made my trek to the post office a bit more labor intensive than usual. Underneath the new snow, the ice-crusted layer shattered with each step, further slowing my progress. It was another cold and gray January in Michigan.

The words to that classic Christmas carol – Good King Wenceslas – kept going through my head. Maybe it's because I had just endured the worst Christmas in my memory.

Good King Wenceslas looked out
On the feast of Stephen
Where the snow lay round about
Deep and crisp and even.

Brightly shone the moon that night
Though the frost was cruel
When a poor man came in sight
Gathering winter fuel.

It wasn't night, but it was pretty darn cold. I felt like that poor man, looking for anything to bring me a small measure of comfort. I refuse to drive my car a half mile to the post office, so come hell or high water, I was walking.

I had a couple of letters to mail: one to the governor to plead my son's case, and another to my son, attempting to deliver love and encouragement.

I've felt like a failure at both lately. Discouragement loves to reach out with its dark, foggy fingers when you least expect it; sucking your breath away and replacing it with a stone – making it hard to breathe. Feeling yourself to be absolutely without resources and hope makes each morning unwelcomed.

I remember when I lived in Arizona – how I loved to be awakened by the sun! I placed my bed just so, and my blinds at the proper level for privacy, but still allowing the sunshine to

The Squeaky Snow and a Boat

kiss my face in the morning. I would get up early to see the sun rise triumphantly over the mountains. I eagerly anticipated each morning as it came. How I loved it there.

Life takes us, abuses us, and casts us into the gutter sometimes.

Gutters are unpleasant places: cold and wet and filthy, with mud and dirt and the detritus of others. When it's hard to breathe, though, we may just lay there for a while, trying to get our strength back. Or, so we tell ourselves. We can become comfortable in our uncomfortableness.

When our hearts have become filled to the brim with hurt and disappointment and despair, we have no room left for light and love and laughter.

We sit in our own filth of depression and weep. We know we need to pick ourselves up and put smiles on our faces. We know we need to let go of what we cannot fix. We know these things.

But grief is a hard taskmaster. Its chains are like hardened steel and all we feel is the pain they inflict whenever we move. So, we try not to move. But they continue to squeeze our filled-up hearts, as if an unseen tormentor was at work; and as the hurt and disappointment and despair spill over, a never-ending well of more keeps seeping in and we don't know how to stop that well up.

So, we stay where we are, restless in our pain, wondering how all the people passing us by don't see us. How they can continue their way as if we aren't there. Our despair makes us mute. And our grief robs us of desire.

I have this mental picture in my head. It's a picture of a small vessel being tossed around on a rough sea. The howling wind and the driving rain are relentless. My tiny boat is slowly swamping and beginning to break apart. Terror is as palpable as the sting of the raindrops on my face. And Jesus is sleeping on a pillow.

And I go to Him and shake Him over and over, begging Him to wake up and help me. But He continues to sleep.

And then I hear some faint words being thrown about on the wind, and they come from

Job long ago – "Though he slay me, yet will I trust him." (Job 13:15 NKJV)

And so here I sit in my proverbial ash heap, proverbially scraping my open sores with pieces of broken pottery as my tears mix with the rain, waiting for Jesus to hear me crying out to Him to wake up.

When our days and nights are dark and terrifying, and when it feels like nothing will ever change for the better, hang on because it will. Despair eventually runs its course and the sharp edges of grief soften.

Plunge into the darkness with the strength you still possess. Fight the demons of doubt and fear. Just as God fed Elijah to strengthen him for his next journey, so God will give you grace to win this battle, no matter how outnumbered you seem to be.

> *Ahab told Jezebel all that Elijah had done, and how he had killed all the prophets with the sword. Then Jezebel sent a messenger to Elijah, saying, "So may the gods do to me and more also,*

if I do not make your life as the life of one of them by this time tomorrow. Then he was afraid, and he arose and ran for his life and came to Beersheba, which belongs to Judah, and left his servant there. But he himself went a day's journey into the wilderness and came and sat down under a broom tree. And he asked that he might die, saying, "It is enough; now, O Lord, take away my life, for I am no better than my fathers." And he lay down and slept under a broom tree. And behold, an angel touched him and said to him, "Arise and eat." And he looked, and behold, there was at his head a cake baked on hot stones and a jar of water. And he ate and drank and lay down again. And the angel of the Lord came again a second time and touched him and said, "Arise and eat, for the journey is too great for you." And he arose and ate and drank and went in the strength of that food forty days and forty nights to Horeb, the mount of God. (I Kings 19:1-8 ESV)

Take courage, for the storm will abate, the sun will shine, and Jesus, through everything, will protect you from the worst of it while you wait. Your strength will grow, and hope will once again spring forth and life will be good.

Trust me. I know. Life will always be difficult, since this is our training ground. Jesus hears us, even when our hearts betray us by believing He is oblivious to our struggles. Believe this — you have protection you can't see and help outside the storm swirling around you, working on your behalf.

It's going to be alright. Hold fast to what you have.

Chapter 5

LIFE IS HARD AND OTHER TRUTHS

I remember I was living in Arizona at the time; I think my second divorce was final by then, but I'm not sure. I was working through a lot of emotional junk, and God had been teaching me about forgiveness and unconditional love. This sunny day, my son called about an accident. The police were accusing him, he told me, of hitting a young woman on her bicycle with his car, killing her, and driving off.

Another parent's nightmare was now entwined with my own and lives would never be the same.

My heart grieved for the young woman and her family; a young life full of promise suddenly gone. I was sorry for my son, who was convinced he hadn't hit her with his car. He would have never knowingly hurt someone and driven off without stopping to help them. It was a terrible blow to all of us, and we weren't sure what was going to happen next.

After the initial flurry of questioning, nothing happened for months. One day, the police showed up at my son's work and arrested him, charging him with vehicular homicide and leaving the scene of an accident with death. I emptied out my meager 401K to help pay for his attorney. He went to trial, was convicted, and sentenced to eleven years in prison. What was his little daughter, only seven years old, going to do without her daddy around? She needed him. We were devastated.

My son had never been in trouble with the law. Ever. This was my baby boy. I still remembered him as an infant in my care. He was the easiest baby ever. He hardly ever cried and was content with wherever you put him or whatever you fed him. He gave me joy.

After he was convicted and sentenced, my emotions went on a roller-coaster ride. I was angry with God that He hadn't stopped this miscarriage of justice, and disappointed in myself that I couldn't somehow "fix" it. I was his mother, after all. It's my job to protect my children no matter their age.

I succumbed to Satan's whispers and lived in a darkness of depression for some months, as you've read about in a previous chapter. My heart was overflowing with despair and sadness. Those were some very dark days, as my eyes could see no glimmer of any light of hope.

By the time he was sentenced to prison, I was living back in Michigan with my parents. I was over 1,000 miles away from Jeremy, so I began writing weekly letters of love and encouragement. I poured myself into those letters, willing the words to somehow reach him and strengthen his heart. This was my only way of hugging him. I wanted him to come back to the Lord and back to his faith.

This is an excerpt from a letter dated April 17, 2013, just a couple of weeks after he was sentenced:

I just read a super awesome book yesterday – Brennan Manning's "The Furious Longing of God." Just, wow! The way he conveys his closeness with Jesus is so very encouraging! Well, he's even closer now, because he just died last week, and I saw his name mentioned on Facebook and decided to check him out. I guess he's mostly known for what I believe was his first book, "The Ragamuffin Gospel."

He talks about how deeply and unswervingly God loves us – individually. The word "furious" he uses is not the fury of anger, but like the fury of a storm at sea. How we are battered around and enveloped in a love that's truly incomprehensible, and then never released; no matter what we do or what we are.

He talks too of how Jesus SAW people – truly saw them – for what they could become and loved them just as they were right there. He saw beyond their shortcomings, lies, cheating, stealing, and mean hearts – and saw the little boy and little girl who needed, more than anything, to know how deeply loved they were right where they were – in the middle of what they were. Beautiful, isn't it?

The Baptist church I grew up in, and a lot of what you kids were taught, I fear, was that, yeah, yeah God loves you, but there is this list, you see, of stuff – I mean you have to conform. You must wear the right clothes and have your hair the right length and say the right buzz words and not do certain things, or else.

When what Jesus told us was this – this is how the world will know that you belong to Me – by the LOVE you have for each other. You know, I never felt overly loved in the churches I grew up in. What about you? I felt I had to fit in, and not let anyone see the real me – the doubting, afraid, hateful, angry, "white-lying" me.

About five years ago, God took me down – all the way down to where all I could do was cry out for help. I'd lost so much, and I felt like I was drowning.

I discovered something then that I'd missed all my life. I encountered a God that zapped me like a lightning bolt with so much love, it has been hard to contain it sometimes. More than forgiveness, more than answering some prayers, it was and still is a connection with a Daddy that has transformed me completely. I never ever want to go back to what I used to be. To know with absolute certainty that the God of the Universe loves me – me! – with an intensity that is beyond anything human – way beyond the depth of love we have for our own children – is staggering. And humbling, and fills me with a joy that is beyond description.

To know and be known by this same Creator who made everything; who cares about everything I'm going through and listens to me always and continually works things out for my good? Well, how can it not change you?

He wants to make us all feel like we are His favorite – special to Him, because we are.

God's Spirit kept reminding me of that Scripture of Jeremiah 29:11, the prophet after whom my son was named – *"I know the plans I have for you. Plans for good and not for evil. To give you a future and a hope."* I clung to those verses like a drowning woman.

In my extreme distress, I remember demanding God give me two things – I wanted my son out of prison, and I wanted him to return to his faith. God said "yes" to the second, and "wait" on the first.

The second, of course, is the most important, but how I want the first as well! As of this writing, we're still waiting.

I moved here to Florida for the express purpose of visiting Jeremy every weekend. It's a five-hour round trip, but I couldn't leave him sitting in prison alone. I just couldn't.

"God is good all the time. All the time God is good."

I must admit it took me a while to really believe those words in my heart. It has taken me many years to acknowledge that God loves my children more than I do, and that He has their best interests in mind. It doesn't mean I don't still ask, well, beg, for God to have my son released. But it does mean I can rest knowing God is in control of the bigger picture.

Why am I writing about this, you're asking? To say that I understand. I can see those hidden places in your heart. Those places you keep sealed up tight so no one can hurt you. Those secrets that bring anxiety and fear. It's ok. Hand them over to the One who understands more than anyone else and let Him begin the healing process.

One day, you'll realize it doesn't hurt so much anymore, and you won't feel the need to explain anymore, and you won't be ashamed anymore.

I wrote down a vision I had some years ago when I was exiting an abusive relationship, and in desperate need of validation.

I see a little girl dancing in a meadow, totally alive to the varied sounds and sights of a breathtakingly beautiful summer day. She whirls and dances with complete abandon, twirling and jumping to a song whose melody only she can hear.

The brightness of the sun is life giving in its warmth.

The colorful meadow flowers are energizing in their sweet scent.

The deep, green grass is long and soft and inviting.

As she moves through the meadow in ever widening slow circles, the flowers bow to her as if to a dance partner – the most beautiful of dance partners. She gently touches their petals of yellow and red and pink and purple and leans down to inhale their incomparably sweet and tantalizing scents. She holds out her hands, a little girl's delicate hands, and laughs with total abandon and unbounded joy.

She pauses for a few moments, waiting expectantly, with anticipation in her hazel eyes. Then she dips and sways to the music of another love song. How does she know it's a love song? Could anything else but a song written just for her bring that bursting joy and tireless desire to dance?

The scene fades.

Knowing you're loved, valuable, and cherished, no matter what happened in the past, is freeing.

Believe it – God loves you as if you were His favorite.

Trust in His timing and trust His heart.

Chapter 6

Sunrise Over the Water

The warmth from the sun reminded me I'd worn the wrong shirt for the weather. The air was cool when I quietly left the house very early this morning in the pre-dawn darkness. Dense fog the color of skim milk was hovering over the ground, muffling all sound.

For many years – most of my adult life – I was terrified of driving in fog. I think it's because it always made me remember an episode from "The Twilight Zone" my mom used to watch. The show came on after my bedtime, but I was sick, so Mom let me stay up with her. Bad idea. Scary things give me nightmares.

But I finally grew up and now the fog doesn't scare me. It just makes me more cautious and introspective.

Every Saturday, my route is the same. Each turn and curve of the road is etched in my memory. My spirit looks forward to experiencing the beauty of the sunrise over the water of the Choctawhatchee Bay as I cross the bridge. This is the highlight of my drive. The pastels in the birthing sky are like a watercolor painting in blues, pinks, and oranges, all seeping together with the colored edges blurring into each other, and the water, sparkling and silvery in the wee hours, a softly rippled mirror.

Peace and serenity and calm: I breathe deeply as I drive into the painting as picturesque as a postcard from paradise, absorbing the sense of the place, letting it snuggle down into my psyche for the day.

Gently undulating back roads and countryside will forever be my favorite way to get from here to there if it's possible. As I enter the Blackwater River State Forest, the curving road, flanked by a pine tree forest lanky with age, follows me for miles as a welcome companion. At random places, the fog softly stretches out from the dense cover of the trees, reaching across the road, dissipating into the foliage on the other side. Cotton fields soon appear, filling the flat farmland; maturing just a little more each week until they're harvested, leaving fluffy handfuls of cotton bolls scrunched up against the sides of the road that look a bit like snow.

I couldn't help myself, and one day I pulled off on the side, got out of my car, and filled my arms with some abandoned cotton leavings. They are soft and white, and I gently pull the fiber out and spin it in my fingers to make thread.

For me, Saturdays are Jeremy days. I have no other plans.

It's a long drive each way, and when I arrive back home in late afternoon, I like to decompress.

The going toward and the leaving behind, every Saturday.

Bittersweet and heart-wrenching. While I'm there, we fill the day with words of encouragement and banter and play card games. He makes his own special recipe of biscuits and gravy we enjoy together, using the meager ingredients available. No shopping or movie-watching. Just sitting in hard chairs, laughing across a long table, sharing the room with many others doing the same. The vending machines work about two-thirds of the time, and sometimes they don't give you your change. You can't complain about anything because the officers might make you leave or, worse, they'll retaliate against my son.

I can only bring myself and some cash and my car key. The rest of my keyring stays in my car. You walk through a metal detector, then around a pole, then you get patted down. Some of the officers are nice and care about the prisoners they watch, and some are awful.

Inside the visiting room, the temperature is freezing in the summer because the thermostat is not in the room where we are, so the air conditioner just keeps running all day. It's even colder in the winter, because there's no real heat to speak of. This prison's buildings are old and not well-maintained, and because it's a prison, nobody cares much. There's never enough money to fix and repair the obsolete buildings. The prisoners don't have any air conditioning, so when the heat reaches the upper 90s it gets unbearable in the dorms.

Sometimes we get to go outside and walk around in the small barb-wire-fenced area, but not often. We do what we can with what we have.

I think most of us have experienced those hard things in life that can suck the joy out of our days.

It's been five years since I began making the weekly drive to see my son in prison. At first, it was heartbreaking to see him incarcerated and treated so poorly, knowing the food he had to eat was not fit for dogs. I often cried all the way home. Then, as the months ambled by and the years began to pile up, we adjusted. We find joy and laughter in simple things now. We're closer than we've ever been. Good memories aren't always made under ideal circumstances, are they?

Remember my lesson on unconditional love I told you about in a previous chapter? This is one of the reasons God needed me to learn it. Unconditional love just keeps on going, even when you feel like you're at the end of what you can do. You set aside what you want to meet the needs of someone else.

> *Then the King will say to those on his right, "Come, you who are blessed by my Father; take your inheritance, the kingdom prepared for you since the creation of the world. For I was hungry, and you gave me something to eat. I was thirsty and you gave me something to drink, I was a stranger and you invited me in, I needed clothes and you clothed me, I was sick and you looked after me, I was in prison and you came to visit me." Then the righteous will answer him, "Lord, when did we see you hungry and feed you, or thirsty and give you something to drink? When did we see you a stranger and invite you in, or needing clothes and clothe you? When did we*

see you sick or in prison and go to visit you?" The King will reply, "I tell you the truth, whatever you did for one of the least of these brothers of mine, you did for me."
(Matthew 25:34-40)

As mothers, we do this automatically for our infants. When those infants become adults, the relationship naturally changes, until a great need arises and out comes the nurturing and giving of ourselves once again until it's no longer needed.

I feel privileged to have been able to be part of my son's spiritual and personal growth, for he's learned a lot of important lessons as well.

But we both long for the day when there will be no more leaving behind.

Because home is where my son will be.

Chapter 7

MY SOMEDAY COUNTRY

It was my first winter back in Michigan after my four-year sojourn in Arizona, and I was homesick for the sunshine and warmth. I had started this new chapter of my life with high hopes of helping and making a difference by serving my parents. After a few months of living in their basement, the reality of the situation zapped me like a violent summer storm. I thrive on sunshine, and my parents' basement, nicely finished and furnished as it was, was devoid of natural light. My psyche took offense by making me feel blue.

Watching my mom lose more of her memory and herself every day, and seeing my dad mourn the loss, was sometimes more than I thought I could bear. This was so hard! Helping someone who doesn't want the help is difficult. My mom had always had trouble understanding what was going on, even before she developed dementia. Now, it seemed all she did was look for a fight. And I knew it wasn't her fault, but the anger and rejection still hurt.

I'm sure you've heard this phrase about someone with dementia: "They aren't giving you a hard time; they're having a hard time," which is true, up to a point. As a caregiver, it usually felt like Momma was giving us a hard time and it's difficult to pretend it's not happening. But, still, it wasn't entirely her fault.

I remember one day I told her how it had hurt me for years watching her do so much more for my sister and my younger brother. She clearly had favorites, and I was the odd child out. She looked at me and said, "It's because you and David (my older brother) aren't special." Wow. I knew what she meant, but those words cut deep. Don't we all want to feel special, especially to our parents?

Living in a house with Mom and Dad filled with childhood reminders on each wall in every room was like traveling back in time. Old feelings shoved down deep for decades bubbled to the surface. I struggled with anger, hurt, and compassion, juxtaposed and jangling against each other. How do I properly care for and love a parent when wrestling with painful memories? Being at once caregiver and needy child took its toll.

But God was gracious, reminding me of the lessons I'd learned such a short time ago.

I linger at the sunroom window, not seeing the view of snow and ice, as my hands cradle my still warm cup of tea. The cold seeps into my bones and I feel like I'll never be warm again. I close my weary eyes, envisioning a someday country in my mind. I let my fertile imagination envelope my senses, and I feel myself going back. Back to a place of sunshine and heat – the kind of heat that makes my skin smell alive.

This, my someday country, has incredible mountain views where I can visit any time I desire. I can gaze longingly on the Watchers from afar, or I can get up close and personal. Climbing through the scrub, up and around the winding trail; resting my hand momentarily on the smooth and warm surface of massive boulders birthed ages ago as I work my way upwards. Stepping carefully around jumping cholla; enthralled at the delicate flowers growing out of rock. Breathing ever more deeply as I work my way up higher and higher, until I can see the way I came from the top of the small mountain. Tears slowly track their way down my cheeks, as my heart is flooded with love for this place. It is a feeling hard to explain.

The warm air is a lover's gentle caress and I want to feel its comfort forever.

There, far below me is the path I took to get here. And farther away in the distance the blue mountains and the snaking road, curving around, finding its way back from where I've come.

As I stand here on my own personal pinnacle, I can feel the beating of my heart slow and the sweat begin to dry on my skin as the breeze moves my hair, bringing coolness to my neck, whispering in my ear.

I linger over the view for some time, drinking in the beauty and the distance and the height. Filling my eyes and my heart with all I see and all I sense and all I hear: the deep, aching azure of the mountains; the smallness of the cars moving along the road; the towering saguaro holding their arms up high as if in praise. There is a peacefulness here that comforts me in my deepest places, healing the wounds obtained from living.

I don't want to leave.

But there is no shelter here; only scraggly mesquite and palo verde trees with scant shade. I sigh deeply and attempt to absorb this place one last time, this moment, etching it forever in my mind and on my heart.

I turn and begin to steadily make my way down the other side, stepping carefully amid the loose stones until I gain the bottom, pausing every so often to listen to the beauty. I feel the history that occurred here. I feel the hopes and laughter and tears of others who left a piece of themselves in this place many years before me. So many who have lived and died here.

I feel their strength and their legacy; their sacrifice and their triumph.

I hear the whisper of the wind again in my ear.

Now I know. I brought my someday country away with me. My mind's eye and my heart are still filled with my mountains and my desert. Because I can never forget, I will always remember. As my heart revisits this place, my memories are etched ever deeper.

As Hebrews 12:1-3 says:

> *Therefore, since we are surrounded by such a great cloud of witnesses, let us throw off everything that hinders and the sin that so easily entangles, and let us run with perseverance the race marked out for us. Let us fix our eyes on Jesus, the author and perfecter of our faith, who for the joy set before him endured the cross, scorning its shame, and sat down at the right hand of the throne of God. Consider him who endured such opposition from sinful men, so that you will not grow weary and lose heart.*

And I now know I can draw on the strength and courage of every traveler who left a part of themselves behind in that beautiful and terrible place still resonating with their life force.

I can hear the wind whispering once again in my ear.

"Do not be afraid. This is the way, walk in it."

God sometimes takes His beloved up rocky paths with dizzying heights and terrifying vistas. We wonder why our lives are not what we expected. We don't know how to fix what seems so broken. We sigh at the window and long for something different than where our paths are currently leading us.

I want to go back. I just want to go back. But our heavenly Father knows what we need and when we need it. Those times of peace and security are made to strengthen our hearts so we can continue to do His will, no matter where He spirits us. Even in places we don't want to be, lessons are there to learn and others that need our help.

As of this writing, I was finally able to go back, for a week at least, to my beloved Arizona after seven long years away. I cried when I left back then and mourned for what I thought I'd lost. But God has been more than faithful, teaching me lessons I wouldn't have been able to learn in Arizona; lessons that are too important to miss.

Always remember, He is making us fit for the kingdom and equipping us to reach out and bring others in with us.

Chapter 8

Wrestling

The months from February of 2013 and into the first few months of 2014 turned out to be one heck of a tough year, to put it mildly. With my son in prison, I needed an outlet for the emotions I was experiencing, so I had started a blog for him, as I've mentioned previously. Writing is an effective way for me to work through painful stuff. It was only by God's grace I made it through December 2013 and January 2014.

My youngest daughter, Bethany, and I were able to drive down to see him for Thanksgiving; and when I realized I wouldn't have the money to get back down to see him for Christmas, well, let's just say I had a total meltdown that lasted for quite a few weeks. With Mom's deteriorating condition, coupled with the stress of being her co-caregiver and having no source of income, it all added to my whole state of mind and heart. But my baby boy's circumstance had taken center stage for me.

My eyes, my heart, my every waking thought was consumed with his situation and my inability to do anything. And I couldn't bear it any longer.

I posted this on his blog right after Christmas:

This Christmas just sucked in many ways. I couldn't seem to get a grip emotionally – spending too many hours crying and wanting to crawl into a hole and be alone. I spent copious hours too, upbraiding God because I finally got angry – at Him.

I kept reminding Him of His promises – and screaming – I want my son back!

Then my youngest daughter let us know about a letter she had just received and suddenly I knew why I had been so distraught. Mothers have emotional connections with their children that is supernatural.

How can our hearts hurt more? We are already broken and bruised – wake up, Jesus! We can't make it to shore on our own.

> *Hey sis, well, this may be the strangest way you've ever received a letter, piggybacking on another one. There's an explanation, have no fear. Here's the short version. I got sent to confinement this past Thursday for fighting. Now, you know me, so you already know I didn't instigate anything. Someone tried to steal my mattress, so I had to fight him for it. And, just for those keeping score at home, I lost ... badly. I had to get some "strips," like fighters get, over my left eye, where I will sport a slight scar until the end of time. So, needless to say, I am at a very low point right now. Luckily, God saw fit to have your letter and Dad's delivered to me the first night I*

was here. So, though they both make me weep, it was also a little encouraging. Thank you for your blog posts; they make me happy and sad at the same time. I'm an emotional mess right now. I've had a rough few weeks, on top of a rough year, and now it's the holidays. The despair and utter desolation that comes over me, sometimes in giant waves, makes it literally (yes literally) hard to breathe.

They don't give you any of your regular property back here, so I'm not sure how soon I'll get writing paper or more envelopes. (Send some please!) I'm not even sure how long I'll be back here, and being a holiday week, it may be longer than normal anyways. So, because I don't have Rachael's address, or ... writing paper, I'm going to send you the blurb for

Mom's Christmas gift from R. ~ Mom, when I think of you, three things come to mind: strong, determined, and morally steadfast. You have shown me, from childhood through the present, how a person who strives to be wise and mature should conduct themselves. You have always been my role model, and I am extremely proud and grateful to be your son.~

I'm not sure if that's what she was looking for or not, so hopefully it works. Please pray for me in earnest as I have been brought so low and need God's guidance and mercy right now. Tell everyone I love them and to write me at my new temporary address for right now.

Your brother, J Paul

Right, as if my heart could hurt any deeper.

One thing I learned – or maybe experienced is a better way to say it, is this – I now know how to wrestle with God. I remember I did a lot of pacing the floor and shaking my fists and screaming, and swearing too. Because I was mad and disappointed and hurt. I distinctly remember telling Jesus He had let me down. I said this more than once. Loudly. Angrily.

And I called Him a liar. I really did. God's patience and forbearance with me is astounding.

For me, the prophet Elijah has always been an intriguing character. I had written some character studies, and the one I wrote about Elijah depicts quite accurately what it is like, at least in my own personal experience, to wrestle with God. Here's a short excerpt:

Thick darkness, a darkness seen with his mind's eye, and felt with this spirit. Like a suffocating black fog. He fought his way through it for a long time. The hours and days passed unknowingly as he wrestled mightily with an unseen but powerful force. He pleaded, he reminded, he worshipped, he held on tightly,

refusing to let go. The words he shouted aloud with growing vehemence were flung back at him, striking deeper into his soul, as if a white-hot blade were cutting him and laying bare his heart. So, he increased his struggles, never giving way once he'd gained some ground. On and on the battle – for that is what it felt like – continued.

Finally, the fog disintegrated, and a calmness stole over his soul. His mind and eyes were clear. He was ready. The training for his next task was complete.

When you've stumbled and crawled through that deep and dark valley of turmoil and grief, I believe that's when you can really get somewhere in your prayers. Not that that's the only time, of course. God hears us in our good times as well as our bad. But for me, the most painful times create for me the best opportunities to really get down and dirty with my heavenly Father. I'm real. I'm in dead earnest. And I'm relentless in my request.

I think – no, I know – God likes it when we're completely engaged and focused. Stop with the mealy-mouthed, phlegmatic prayers. He's not impressed.

But in order to get there and to the other side, I had to go through brutal days and weeks.

So, what I've learned is this – don't ever be afraid to tell God how you feel and what you need. He can handle your anger, your sadness, and your ridiculousness. He can turn your heart in the right direction, so your desires begin to align with His. He is neither hindered nor appalled at your feelings, or your choice of words.

So, let loose. Just be real. And be prepared to be changed. You will not be the same afterward.

Trust me. I know.

> "The point of defeat – the urge to throw up your hands and surrender – seems like the most desolate corner of creation. It actually places you in prime

position to experience God's strength and provision because, as it turns out, God is drawn to the desperate. If you trace this idea in Scripture, you'll find that God's deliverance often follows closely upon a time of desperation. His blessing tends to fall upon a condition of brokenness. Throughout history, his most powerful servants have all come from a place of desolation and defeat." (Idleman, 2019)

Chapter 9

A Lesson from Habakkuk

"Though the fig tree should not blossom,
   nor fruit be on the vines,
the produce of the olive fail
   and the fields yield no food,
the flock be cut off from the fold
   and there be no herd in the stalls,
yet I will rejoice in the Lord.

   I will take joy in the God of my salvation.
God, the Lord, is my strength;
   he makes my feet like the deer's;
he makes me tread on my high places."

Habakkuk 3:17-19, ESV

Life was about to get much worse for Habakkuk's people, the nation of Israel. Chaldean forces would arrive, raze Jerusalem, and take its people captive to a foreign land:

raping, pillaging, enslaving. Habakkuk's people, forced to leave their homes, would live where they didn't want to live, forced to endure what they didn't want to endure.

Scholars say Habakkuk was a contemporary of the prophet Jeremiah, who also warned the Jews of God's coming judgment for their sin. (Wikipedia).

Life gets hard and we become discouraged. We pray and our circumstances don't improve. We beg and God's silence is deafening.

Our needs are great and we cry out to our Father to provide, and He seems to ignore our pleadings. We plod through our days with our hearts downtrodden and bruised. We seek rest, peace, and restoration. We want an end to our suffering.

The Israelites were exiles in Babylon for seventy years before they could return to Jerusalem. They returned to a destroyed city, whose walls were broken down and where wild animals had made their homes. With enemies all around them, they set out to rebuild their walls and their city, while prepared to fight for their lives. (Nehemiah chapter 4).

The days and decades were terrible, difficult, and painful and seemed never-ending.

And yet, the heart-cry of God's faithful people will always be "even though – even though, I will rejoice..." Even though my child is sick. Even though my house is damaged and in desperate need of repair. Even though my bank account is empty. Even though my spouse is dead.

With our eyes fixed on Jesus, the author and finisher of our faith, we can be confident in knowing the ending of the story will always be a happy one.

"I am coming quickly; hold fast to what you have, so that no one will take your crown." (Revelation 3:11, NASB, church of Philadelphia)

Our Father is always listening. He hears and cares. Sometimes He says "yes"; sometimes He says "no"; and sometimes He says, "not yet."

When your difficult days seem to go on and on without relief, remember that all we can see is our small world, but God sees it in its entirety. His plans will unfold in due time, and during your difficulty, He will send small mercies your way to encourage your heart and show you just how much He really loves you.

Section Two

FORGIVENESS

Jess and the Sparrow

The chains were too tight. They threatened to cut off her breath. Jess kept waiting for her tormentor to let her go.

"Please!" she begged, "I have nothing more to give you!"

She slowly sank down to the ground in her small, dark cage and leaned her back against the cold bars. Drawing her knees up to shield her face, she sobbed out her grief. How long has she been here? She had lost track of time. The days and nights crept forward, never halting, and without illumination.

She knew she had been here for many days.

There was a tiny opening in the stone wall up near the ceiling that let in air and just a hint of light sometimes.

Would her little friend stop by to visit again today? He was just a sparrow, but she really looked forward to hearing him pecking around outside her window.

Just yesterday, she thought she heard him speaking to her. I'm getting delusional, she thought.

But she distinctly remembered his squeaky whispers.

"Let it go." That's what she heard. It echoed in her mind and she couldn't shut out the voice. Was that really what he said?

No, that can't be right. What could she let go of? She was chained here – a prisoner.

"Jess, Jess!"

Who is there? Was it her little friend again today?

"I can hear you, little sparrow!" *Oh, dear God please don't let me be losing my mind!* Jess thought.

"I have the key for you, Jess!"

Those squeaky whispers made her heart leap for joy.

"Where is it? I'm right here!" A sob caught in her throat as her hope awakened.

"You must listen ever so carefully, ok?"

"Ok!"

"Let it go."

"What?"

"Let it go. Forgive."
"What?!"
"Let it go. Forgive."

Her new hope withered and died, just like that. Clearly, she was delusional. Let go of what? And forgive who? Surely, he wasn't suggesting she forgive her tormentor.

Out of the question! How could she forgive the very one inflicting pain on her day in and day out? No one should be expected to do that.

By the time she came to herself, her little friend had left.

She felt lonelier and more abandoned than she had ever felt in her life. Even her little friend mocked her pain.

But his words drilled themselves deep down inside her heart, and became a mantra.

Three days later, after listening to this mantra almost non-stop, she heard her little friend outside.

But, wait, it sounded different.

"Are you there, little friend?"

"Don't listen to him – you've been wronged! You need justice and revenge! Don't listen to him!"

"Who are you?"

"Hold tightly and never forgive, and never forget!"

"Wait! What?"

She heard a slithering sound and then silence.

Confusion filled her heart. *Oh, please, I just want my little friend back! Please!*

She threw herself down to the filthy, dirt floor and cried out her frustration and conflict. After a while, she became calm. Her thoughts drifted and she began to remember.

There were some good times. Yes, that's true. They weren't all bad. Her thoughts went farther back in time, back beyond her own personal knowledge of events. She saw her tormentor as a child. Then as a young person. Then as an adult. She saw things and her heart warmed to this person who had experienced their own brand of hurt.

And she began to understand.

"Hi, Jess!" Whispered her little friend. She could hear a smile in his voice today.

"Are you ready to use your key?" he said to her.

"Yes, oh, yes!" She cried out.

"Wonderful! I'll see you outside then. It's a beautiful day here – come on!"

Her little friend was so right – it was a gorgeously beautiful day, and Jess, with her arms lifted high, danced around and around until she fell to the ground laughing, inhaling the sweet scent of the flowers.

Forgiveness – Why is It So Difficult?

Forgiveness – it's such a hard thing to do. Betrayal hurts. Disappointment in others and in ourselves is like dealing with a clogged drain. We're stuck. We often feel justified in our anger, disappointment, and betrayal, making excuses we disingenuously refer to as good reasons for our behavior.

Feeling "righteously angry" is intoxicating. We can easily justify our decisions when we feel so empowered. Bitterness gets a foothold and grows like a toxic weed in a cultivated garden, choking out the more delicate plants until all that is left is an untended tangle of unwanted growth needing to be eradicated.

When you think about it, forgiving others is easier than forgiving ourselves, isn't it? We can learn to empathize with the one who hurt us initially and learn to forgive them, and even restore broken relationships.

But forgiving ourselves is much harder. How do we learn to empathize with ourselves instead of blaming ourselves for what happened? How do we come to grips with our failings and accept ourselves for the frail but still valuable people we are?

Remember how the apostle Peter, in Matthew 26:75, after denying Jesus three times, wept bitterly? Remember, too, how Jesus forgave him? Peter went on to be one of the greats in history, proclaiming the gospel to everyone, primarily the Jewish people, to whom he was called. God used him to spread the good news and bring many to Christ.

What about Paul, whose name was originally Saul? Saul the Persecutor they called him. One day, Jesus knocked him off his donkey and gave him a new heart. Throughout the last 2,000 years, the Apostle Paul's letters have been used by God to bring countless millions of souls into the kingdom.

These two men could have spent the rest of their lives wallowing in their guilt. Instead, they chose to forgive themselves, once they were forgiven by God, and become great men of faith.

Satan loves to keep us stuck, thereby rendering us ineffective. His lies tell us we're not good enough to be forgiven: that we've been too bad, done too much, hurt too many. Sure, he tells us, God may forgive you, but you can't ever forgive yourself – that's what will keep you humble. If you forgive yourself, you may become prideful and that's a bad thing.

Yes, it is. Pride is a very bad thing. However, the lie is in what forgiving yourself accomplishes for you. It doesn't make you prideful; it makes you thankful and, in turn, usable.

God's purpose for keeping His children here on earth is to use us to bring in the rest of the sheep, and to encourage our brothers and sisters. We can't do that well when we're trapped in a cage of our own making.

The process of forgiveness may be a long journey, but it's a necessary one.

Godspeed!

Chapter 1

Forgiving Ourselves

I had just weaned my ten-month-old, a curly-haired, cupid-faced baby, and discovered I was pregnant again. I wasn't ready for another baby. I loved my little Rachael with my whole heart and didn't want to go through another pregnancy so soon. My heart was already full; plus, I had just gotten my girlish figure back.

Being an extreme introvert, and getting married not long after graduating high school, I had no forewarning of the necessary changes that would occur having a husband and baby. My personal time that had been so important to me was mostly non-existent now, what with running a household, keeping my husband happy, and my baby healthy. I was happy too, until I realized I was going to have another baby to take care of.

My upbringing hadn't really prepared me for this, and I apparently hadn't read enough books on the proper subject of being a good mother. I had very little counsel from my mom, because things just weren't discussed. And growing up in a household where emotions were masked, I kept most things to myself and worked through them on my own. Unfortunately, this same upbringing, and the Baptist churches I was raised in, didn't focus on a very important concept.

I was a Christian and read my Bible daily. But I had never learned the importance of taking everything to my heavenly Father and, even more so, never learned how to do it. I thought I had to figure it all out on my own which, to my detriment, was a huge mistake. I can't blame anyone else for this. I might not have been taught it, but that didn't absolve me of the responsibility to learn it for myself.

I didn't understand what Jesus meant when He said, *"Come to me, all you who are weary and burdened, and I will give you rest."* *(Matthew 11:28)* My life was humming along nicely, so I didn't see that I needed what He was offering; that was for other people. I had a brain and I was prepared to use it. And the idea of relinquishing control over any aspect of my life was scary.

Instead of being thankful for the growing life inside me, I was irritated. I did not want another baby to infringe even more on my limited personal time. Wasn't one baby enough? To say I had a bad attitude would be to put it mildly. The older I get, the more I see the prima donna in my mom come out in me, and it makes me cringe.

From the beginning of the pregnancy, I didn't physically feel quite right. I couldn't put my finger on it exactly, but something felt "off" somehow. Not wanting to be pregnant, of course, wasn't helping me out physically or mentally.

At about twelve weeks along, God decided I wasn't worthy to love this baby and He took it from me. I had a miscarriage and the guilt of feeling like I had killed my own baby, even if it was only in my heart, haunted me for many years. Forgiving ourselves is a monumental task indeed.

Several months after my miscarriage, I became pregnant with my son, Jeremy, and feared, during the entire nine months, that I would lose him too. By now, I really wanted a baby. And God granted me mercy and gave me a healthy son. Then three years later, I became pregnant again and went through a similar gamut of feelings of not wanting a third child. I had two healthy babies now, and I was content and didn't want or need another one. Thanks, God, but no thanks.

If I had a nickel for every time I thought I knew better than God, I'd be rich. He is so patient with me; it makes me ashamed to admit it.

With this pregnancy, though, I checked my frustration, and once I felt the baby move inside me, I loved her as much as I did my other two. God was overwhelmingly gracious and saw fit to gift me with Bethany, the child who has been there over the years in more ways than I can count for her momma who, at the beginning, didn't want her. Well, I should qualify that statement a little. It wasn't her I didn't want. I didn't know her; it was a third baby to take care of I didn't want. But still, semantics, right?

Forgiving others is a difficult thing. Forgiving ourselves can be as tough as climbing Mount Everest with no training or the right equipment. You've failed before you've begun.

I enjoy some of the Facebook memes out there, and one of them goes something like this: *You can visit your past, but remember, you don't live there anymore.*

You ask for forgiveness, accept it, then move on. The only times you should be revisiting the grave of a miscarried or aborted child is when you either need a reminder of God's grace, or when you need to reach down and lift another woman up. You visit a grave; you don't pitch a tent and live there.

Satan wants us to live our lives immersed and trapped inside our past mistakes. The accusations, the guilt, the shame: these prevent us from doing the good works God has prepared for us to do.

> *"...Forgetting what is behind and straining toward what is ahead, I press on toward the goal to win the prize for which God has called me heavenward in Christ Jesus."*
> *(Philippians 3:13-14)*

We may beat ourselves up over the past and others may refuse to let us forget, stripping us of our dignity and self-worth, but God treats us differently. Once we are forgiven, He allows us to move forward, gives us grace after grace along the way, and equips us to encourage others in their journeys.

I love Brennan Manning's books. In *The Ragamuffin Gospel*, he says this about grace and how we've distorted it into something it isn't.

> "Though the Scriptures insist on God's initiative in the work of salvation – that by grace we are saved, that the Tremendous Lover has taken to the chase – our spirituality often starts with self,

not God. Personal responsibility has replaced personal response. We talk about acquiring virtue as if it were a skill that can be attained, like good handwriting or a well-grooved golf swing...The emphasis is on what I do rather than on what God is doing...We believe that we can pull ourselves up by our bootstraps – indeed, we can do it ourselves...Sooner or later we are confronted with the painful truth of our inadequacy and insufficiency. Our security is shattered, and our bootstraps are cut." (Manning, 1990)

I'm finally beginning to understand grace. God has given me so much more than I deserve: children, grandchildren, friends, and opportunities to be a light in someone else's darkness.

There is no more room for shame or guilt.

He loves you, and as He gazes upon you, He sees you through the blood of His sinless Son, and you are justified. You're no longer guilty.

His beloved child.

I birthed three living children, but I am a biological mother of four. I accept this and look forward to the day in heaven when I will meet this little one for the first time. And all there will be is love.

Chapter 2

Divorce One

The wedding gown was simple, elegant, and lovingly made by my mom. It was beautiful. Mom had become an excellent seamstress over the years, teaching herself to make a variety of garments. The veil cost twice as much as the material for the dress. It was a cold and dreary November afternoon, but it didn't matter about the weather. This was my wedding day, and I was happy. My bouquet was full of roses and my life, I felt, was just beginning; the start of my happily ever after.

I had dreamed about this day ever since I was a little girl. My prince had come, and now the day had finally arrived.

If only I'd known what the future held, would I have walked down that aisle or run away? I would have run for sure, fast and far.

Marrying a narcissist and a controlling, manipulative person doesn't bode well for any marriage. I'm not saying they can't work. I do know mine didn't.

The happy day, unfortunately, didn't last so very long. And as the years piled up, they grew progressively worse.

There were happy days, no doubt about it. I remember he used to refer to himself as my "knight in tarnished armor." As is true in every marriage, no matter how difficult, nothing is ever totally horrible. But the whiplash of his approval then disapproval, back and forth repeatedly, finally wore me down.

Three children and nineteen years later, I couldn't take anymore. My health was suffering from the stress of waiting for the next explosion, which was never far off. My weight had dropped so much I looked like a scrawny chicken. Each evening around 11:30 pm, about the time I knew he'd be getting home from work (he worked a second shift in the shop for General Motors), I would begin to tremble all over, casting back in my mind everything that had happened that day to see if I'd missed anything that might make him angry. Did I leave a window open? Did I forget to attach an errant downspout the wind had dislodged? Was there a toy or tool lying around?

What would he ask me about tonight that would send him into a rage? The kids and I hid things from him out of self-preservation. We conspired together and were like brothers in arms in a foxhole. I never knew what would set him off and was always on the defensive, which put me in a very bad position. When he flew into one of his rages, it felt like being flayed with a whip. The beating was all verbal. I could see myself emotionally bleeding out, with pieces of me lying all over the floor. This was my daily torture session.

Our nightmare, and I included my three children in this, had been recurring for a long time. But our friends at church didn't know. He put up a good front there. He said the right things and prayed the right prayers. We even helped lead worship – I played piano and he played guitar.

But there's only so much a person can take.

Our marriage finally and irrevocably ended the day he threatened my oldest daughter, who was eighteen at the time, with physical violence over a burned bagel of all things. It's a crazy and stupid story, but it was the straw that broke the camel's back for me. I confronted him and he kicked me out.

What he didn't know was that I had made sure the kids were elsewhere when I stood up to him, as he arrived home from work that night, because I wasn't sure how he would react. He had quite an extensive gun and knife collection, so I didn't know if I'd come out of it alive. But enough was enough.

That was the beginning of a brand-new nightmare.

And for many months, I was angry with God. Do you sense a pattern in my behavior? When I don't get what I want, I become petulant and angry. I blamed him for my marriage falling apart. I kept reminding him that I was a "good girl," an obedient wife, and good mother.

For some reason, even though I had been raised in a Baptist home and knew the Bible quite well, I had this idea in my head that if I was "good enough," then things had to work out for me; that God would make sure I had my happily ever after. Apparently, I was wrong. Life was not like one of my favorite fairy-tale stories.

During the whole horrible divorce process, all seventeen agonizing months of it, I sank deeper and deeper into a depression of hopelessness. I couldn't see a way out. I wasn't supposed to get a divorce. Now, for the first time in my life, I was on the outside looking in, and I didn't particularly like what I saw or how the rejection felt. These were my brothers and sisters in Christ. But most of them backed away as if I had leprosy. I was left, for all intents and purposes, alone to pick up the pieces of my broken and shattered life.

I was raised in church. Even though we didn't have a list, per se, of rules, we all knew what they were. And getting a divorce was a huge no-no. Suddenly, my motives were suspect. Why was I really getting a divorce? Was I having an affair? If I got a new haircut, it might mean I was trolling for another husband. And the tongues would wag.

It was awful.

But one day, God said something to me I've never forgotten, and it changed my life. "My job isn't to make you happy. Your job is to worship me, no matter what happens."

Those words stopped me cold. I began to think about that statement, and in doing so, my heart began to change. It took a long time to forgive my first husband, but with God's grace it did happen.

My forgiveness, though, didn't come about because I took the time to look at things from my ex-husband's perspective. I didn't like his perspective. He was mean and nasty, as far as I was concerned. The forgiveness I was able to give was all because my heavenly Father helped me understand a very important truth.

What my husband did to me and our children wasn't the important thing. What I did with the anger, disappointment, and hurt was.

> *"[W]ho comforts us in all our affliction, so that we may be able to*

> *comfort those who are in any affliction, with the comfort with which we ourselves are comforted by God."* (II Corinthians 1:4, ESV)

I learned to have compassion and empathy for others who were on the outside, because I got a good taste of how it feels. Before my divorce, I had little tolerance for anyone different than myself. My world view was very small, but it was all I had; so to me, it was all-encompassing.

Jesus has given me the opportunity to participate in others' pain, and it's made me a better person for it.

So, I can't be angry anymore with my ex-husband. I don't dwell on the nightmares of the past. Now, I keep my eyes open to others who are hurting like I was and try to bring them encouragement.

In my darkest days and nights, when I felt God had abandoned me, He was equipping me for good works. How can I be angry about such a wonderful outcome?

I can now show my scars to another woman going through a similar situation. See, we're sisters. We can do this together. God got me through it, and He'll get you through it too.

Chapter 3

When Forgiveness Hurts Too Much

I was quite sure I had that forgiveness thing well under control after my four-year Arizona solitude. I had learned much and had practiced what I'd been taught.

Check that one off my list! Got it down pat. Oh, yeah.

Oh no, I didn't.

For those last eighteen months or so that I lived in Arizona, when I would call every week to talk with my folks, I began to hear something in my dad's voice. He told me one day he'd taken Mom to the doctor. The doctor informed them Mom had dementia, the early stages; possibly Alzheimer's. As you can imagine, it was quite a blow.

But he didn't ask me for help. Of course, he never would. My parents are the perfect examples of doing everything themselves. But I knew; I listened between the lines, so to speak.

An idea began to form, then take root, and grow over a period of months. During this time, I had gotten my hands on several books, reading them one after another, as is my way of consuming the printed word when I'm in a reading mood.

There were three books God used to gradually open my heart to answer his call to serve my parents. The first was Don Miller's sequel to his very popular *Blue Like Jazz,* entitled *A Million Miles in a Thousand Years.* I couldn't get the idea of starting a "new story" out of my thoughts. Then there was Max Lucado's newest book *Outlive Your Life.* His words about doing and being more resonated with me. Then the last one was Richard Paul Evan's novel *The Walk.* I felt like I was at a crossroads in my life too, just like the main character's.

God was making me restless in my safe, comfortable life. I was making plenty of money to pay my bills and fly to Michigan to visit my parents a couple times a year. But suddenly it wasn't what I wanted. I didn't want safe. I wanted to do something scary and risky for God. I wanted my life to count for something special; something more than making money in a career; something of lasting significance.

Jesus spoke of this in Matthew, as part of the Beatitudes.

> *Do not store up for yourselves treasures on earth, where moths and vermin destroy, and where thieves break in and steal. But store up for yourselves treasures in heaven, where moths and vermin do not destroy, and where thieves do not break in and steal. For where your treasure is, there your heart will be also. (Matthew 6:19-21)*

After much prayer and meditation, I ended up resigning from my position at work, selling some and giving most of my furniture away, then shoving my few remaining worldly possessions back into my car, and driving across the country again – this time in the opposite direction – to live in my parents' basement and to help my dad with my mom, so he wouldn't have to bear the burden all alone.

Fun times it ain't. Well, some of the time it was. The feeling of being part of a family unit again was nice. I had forgotten, since my children were all grown and on their own, what it was like having other people in your household care about where you were and what you were doing. And when I first moved in, Mom's condition was still in its early stages. So, she was happy to have me there and we had some pleasant conversations while she was still able to understand what was going on.

I never saw her cry about her diagnosis. It made her sad, but her typical stoic self, held the fear and sadness inside so it was not spoken of, and I wish it had been. When we can put a voice to our fears and will trust those closest to us with our deepest pain, it can ease everyone's burdens. We can mourn together. But even then, with such abysmal news, she kept her thoughts and feelings to herself.

And as we daily observed Mom's slow slide, Dad and I discovered just how brutal of a diagnosis dementia is. The daily watching hurts like the dickens. As her condition worsened, I would occasionally write something:

The kitchen was always Momma's domain. Her wonderful, southern cooking was known far and wide among not just family, but my kids' friends as well.

Big pots of homemade beef stew, along with the best cornbread baked in her cast iron skillet – seasoned with bacon grease. Creamy mashed potatoes worth fighting over. No one could enter her house without being pressed to have something to eat: biscuits, green beans, baked chicken, apple pies, cakes and

cookies, just for starters.

She doesn't remember how to cook anymore. She doesn't remember much about specific foods either. Names of ingredients mean nothing. Spices are things she doesn't understand. Her taste buds keep changing what they like and don't like.

At dinner, Dad and I put the food portions on her plate for her. She sits and looks for a few moments, uncomprehending, at the food in front of her. She picks up her knife, sticks it in in her salad, then puts it back down. She picks up her fork and waves it around confusedly, not sure what to do with it.

"Here, Momma," I say, "your salad dressing goes here, on your salad. You don't want it on your meatloaf, trust me." But she doesn't know the difference between her meatloaf and her salad. So, I gently take the salad dressing bottle away from her and pour it over her salad for her. "There you go! I think you'll like that much better!"

Each dinner is an exercise in patience. Each dinner reveals our sadness at the loss of so much. But my dad perseveres. He is the epitome of bravery to me.

A few months after settling in, I had the misfortune of watching Mom work herself up into one of her rages where her tongue became a lethal weapon. She did this on a regular basis. Dad told me that she'd been like that for decades and he'd just had to put up with it. His doctor had prescribed a mild anti-depressive years ago that he'd been taking. And with the dementia, it became a whole lot worse.

Then, of course, after a few more months, she felt comfortable enough to include me in her fits of nastiness.

It brought back some very painful memories I had suppressed way down deep. It also slapped me in the face with the reason I had spent much of my childhood immersed in one book after another. I lived in other stories – stories that had happy endings. And if they didn't have an ending good enough to satisfy me, then I rewrote it so that it did.

For me, life had to have a happy ending. It was non-negotiable.

One day, my heart finally saw what I hadn't wanted to see. My mom's brand of love was controlling, manipulative, and conditional. But how was I to recognize something so destructive as a child? And what could I have done about it anyway? Now here I am two abusive husbands and two divorces later. Thanks, Mom.

I was learning a whole new aspect of forgiveness. And there were many days I just didn't want to cooperate. This pain went all the way back to my beginnings, to the very core of who I was. The person who was supposed to love me unconditionally didn't. What do you do with that kind of brokenness?

I've mentioned before that my modus operandi for protecting myself was to emotionally retreat. This has been a most difficult habit for me to break. I had to become attuned to the triggers and to have a game plan all worked out on how to handle the situation.

Part of my game plan was to set some boundaries. And they worked. Mom didn't appreciate them, but I did.

Forgiveness is freeing, though. But the process of forgiving a parent is so very painful.

I first had to allow myself to acknowledge what had happened. Then I had to try and understand why my mom was the way she was. I needed some perspective. I did a lot of whining and crying. I got sick of it myself, and I know my kids got tired of hearing it from me, too. But, you know, grief is a journey; a twisty-turny kind of journey where you can easily get lost. It takes time working through issues. And that's alright.

Just remember your goal: Forgiveness.

I will acknowledge there were some happy times: days when Momma was a bit like who she used to be, telling jokes and laughing at them; days when she kind of remembered her grandchildren, or at least some of them; days when she was happy remembering things that happened years ago; and even days when she said something motherly to me – catching me by surprise. Like the day she told me, in a very round-about way, she just wanted me to be happy when I told her a bit about my heartbreak over a guy friend. She had seen my tears when I tried to hide them. So, yeah, there were some good days for sure.

Perspective is one part of the forgiveness process. Once we begin to understand what shaped this person who has hurt us, our natural empathy will kick in and we'll see the end of the journey not too far in the distance.

I'd like to close this chapter with a passage from Bob Goff's newest best-seller *Everybody*

Always. If you haven't read it yet, you need to. It's life-changing. He writes in one chapter about how to love difficult people. Here's a portion:

> When I meet someone who is hard to get along with, I think, *Can I love that person for the next thirty seconds?* While they continue to irritate me, I find myself counting silently...*twenty-seven, twenty-eight, twenty-nine*... and before I get to thirty, I say to myself, *Okay, I'm going to love that person for thirty more seconds.* This is what I've been doing with the difficult commands of Jesus too. Instead of agreeing with all of them, I'm trying to obey God for thirty seconds at a time and live into them. I try to love the person in front of me the way Jesus did for the next thirty seconds rather than merely agree with Jesus and

avoid them entirely, which I'm sad to say comes easier to me. I try to see difficult people in front of me for who they could become someday, and I keep reminding myself about this possibility for thirty seconds at a time.

It's easy to agree with what Jesus said. What's hard is actually doing what Jesus did. For me, agreeing is cheap and obeying is costly. Obeying is costly because it's uncomfortable. It makes me grow one decision and one discussion at a time. It makes me put away my pride. These are the kinds of decisions that aren't made once for a lifetime; they're made thirty seconds at a time. (Goff, 2018)

See, I told you he was good. If you need to practice forgiveness thirty seconds at a time, then do it. Just do it.

Chapter 4

The Hike

Forgiving others for hurting us is one thing. Forgiving others for hurting someone we love is something else altogether, or so we think. How many times have we justified our unforgiving spirits when our loved ones have been injured?

My mom, bless her heart, had this capacity for holding onto anger that would have won her an Olympic medal if it had been considered a sport. She was like a pit bull – grabbing on and never letting go. Case in point: Way back many decades ago, when my older brother was a teenager, he fell in love with a beautiful, blonde-haired girl with an infectious laugh. He was over the moon for her, as they say. They dated for some months and then one day she dumped him for someone else and, even though he finally recovered, my mom never did. I think she went to her grave still angry at not just the girl, but her whole family. That's the power of a grudge. I found out not too many years ago that my mom (and me by birth) are related to the Hatfields and the McCoys, for real. You see what I'm up against.

A similar thing happened to me when someone deeply hurt one of my children and I broke off the family ties completely. I told them I never wanted to speak to them again. I was "righteously angry." No, I was just angry. And after many months of brooding and feeling justified in my decision, God had a talk with me, again, about forgiveness, because I apparently hadn't learned that lesson well enough yet. I had, up to that point, refused to listen to even my dad's counsel. And that's saying a lot, because I've always valued his opinion and wisdom.

When I really need to ruminate on something, I go for a walk if possible. The lessons nature teaches are poignant and heart-changing. In Florida, since I live so close to the ocean, I go for a walk along the beach and let the frothing water tickle my ankles, drink in the vast horizon, and watch the sun sink below the water, and let it calm my spirit.

When I lived in Arizona, I'd go for a walk in the desert or mountains when I had something especially heavy weighing on my heart that needed to be worked through. The physical aspect of the hike would get the blood pumping so I could think more clearly and commune with God in solitude, and the scenery would soothe my soul. Each critter and plant lived together in harmony, and I reveled in the beauty of it all.

The suffocating heat is oppressive. The sun's beat-down makes me wish I'd started my hike earlier in the day. I was almost there, but that last mile was brutal.

I pause for a few minutes in the shade of a mesquite tree to catch my breath and drink from my water bottle. The water is quite warm now, but it's wet and that's what matters. My gaze seeks out the distant blue mountains, appearing closer than they are. I breathe deeply and allow my mind to rest, and I smile. The immediate scenery at my feet is brown and tan and varying shades of green, with the occasional flowering shrub bravely brightening the landscape.

Tough. Patient. Resilient. Forgiving. These words describe the Arizona desert's flora and fauna.

My back is covered in sweat and I can feel lines of moisture slowly tracking down my neck, even as the wind lifts my hair to bring a teaser of coolness. Even with the extreme heat and sweating, my skin dries quickly because of the low humidity.

The never-ending bright, blue sky remains, and only yields grudgingly to the evening by changing colors ever so slowly. The last half hour of light the sky explodes into neon orange as if the blue suddenly relinquishes all hold to the day and bids us a farewell.

I pass by an acacia tree in bloom whose honey-sweet scent greets me, making me slow my steps and turn in my tracks for just a few moments to relish the beauty of sweetness hovering in the heated air. I gently finger a soft, fuzzy golden yellow ball of scent before I move on. The heat is intensifying and I'm getting tired. My strength is flagging, and the memory of my morning exuberance is a distant mirage.

I walk reverently by a tortoise posing as a statue, his movements agonizingly slow and deliberate. Tiny lizards silently fly across the ground, disappearing into the scrub on some errand of extreme importance and immediacy.

Cactus wrens remain perched up high, peeking outside the nesting holes they carved into the saguaro's flesh up near the top, their young safe from predators. Their little ones strategically surrounded by razor sharp cactus spines chirp out their hunger and wait.

A road runner streaks past, leaving a dust trail in his wake, agilely weaving around the scrub and cholla and small boulders strewn throughout the landscape like marbles that have fallen out of a bag and disappears down the path in a tumble of pebbles.

Life in the desert is precarious, with each day bringing its own portent of possible disaster. It's also patient, forgiving, and resolute. Single-mindedness of survival, with the summer day beginning hot and increasing in its merciless heat until the earth incrementally turns and the sun sets. The night becomes almost cool and the air a caress, as if apologizing for the inhospitable day.

The blackness of the night shrouds the mountains in a cloak of secrecy, where they appear in the morning light again like a wayward lover with a kiss of welcome.

The saguaro teaches me how to forgive the birds for disfiguring their faces because their babies need shelter, and the cactus flowers teach me how to appreciate even the painful spines of disappointment still finding a way to bloom. The tortoise's patient forward movement reminds me to "hamba gashle" or make haste slowly. The small trees with their tiny leaves and bright flowers tell me to be thankful for the refreshing rain when it finally arrives. They don't harbor resentment for the lack but cherish each drop as it falls.

When I cast back in my memory for the untold times God has forgiven me, how can I really hold on to anger against someone else? I've messed up too many times to count and He's never once said – nope, I'm not forgiving you again. Which begs the question

– who do we think we are when we say that to someone else?

Jesus's words in the passage of Scripture we refer to as the Beatitudes are beautifully poetic. *"Blessed are the merciful, for they will obtain mercy." (Matthew 5:7)*

And then again, when answering His disciples' question about how many times we must forgive a brother: *"seventy times seven." (Matthew 18:22)* I'm thinking Jesus was trying to say, "Don't hold onto it; let it go." In the big picture, those irritations mean nothing.

And Jesus, while on the cross paying the price for our sins, refused to harbor bitterness toward His executioners and said, *"Father, forgive them, for they know not what they do." (Luke 23:34)*

I know I've said it before, but it bears repeating. Forgiveness is always a choice. It might not seem so at the time, but it is. And for you readers still holding tightly to your anger, that just made you a little angrier, didn't it? Remember, I know how it feels.

If someone wrote me into a novel, what would be my character traits? How would they describe me to their readers? How would they describe you?

I desire to be known for my forgiving spirit and not my ability to harbor anger; to be someone approachable and gentle in heart. I want my character to be someone who, once she was gone, would be fondly missed.

The chains we forge by our anger hurt us the most. When we feel like we just can't forgive, God reminds us that we can. And that we must.

"But if you do not forgive others their sins, your Father will not forgive your sins." (Matthew 6:15)

Take a good, long walk in nature and let God open your eyes to the thankfulness and forgiveness all around you in His creation. Work at keeping things in their proper perspectives.

Have you started practicing the thirty-second rule yet?

Chapter 5

Jonah's Legacy

I incrementally allowed myself to adopt the mindset of thinking God was responsible for making me happy again. Months trudged by and I sank into a period of deep depression where I wanted to die. I was done. My inability to fix the monumental problem, coupled with my guilt of not being a good mother, overwhelmed me. What should I have done differently? I just didn't know.

In the book of Jonah, you'll notice the prophet never recovered from his depression. He started out angry and stubborn, and ended his story angry and stubborn.

Can God only use us when we're all shiny and clean? Jonah's a great example of a typical man with baggage and an unforgiving heart. He hated the Ninevites for what they'd done to his people. He may have had direct family members killed by them. We don't know the details, but we feel his deep-seated hatred.

God saw Jonah and picked him to deliver a message of life and deliverance. *"Love your enemies,"* Jesus told us. *"Do good to those who persecute you." (Matthew 5:44)*

Did Jonah feel chained to his anger like I did? Did he really believe saying no to God was going to end well for him? Did he care? Probably not.

I wrote a character study on Jonah a few years back. I've included it here.

How he hated them! He loathed them to the point of flat-out refusing to deliver a time-sensitive message of mercy.

Why should he help them at all? After everything they've done. "No," he thought, "I won't do it. No matter what God says. I can't forgive. I just can't."

Jonah located a ship, bought his ticket, and left for somewhere in the opposite direction of Nineveh. Tarshish would do nicely.

Jonah kept glancing over his shoulder as he hurried toward the ship that would take him far away from "those people." He stumbled on the dock in his haste and nervousness. No way would he give any sort of help at all – "not in my lifetime," he thought. His pent-up hatred, always simmering below the surface, bubbled up into a feeling so fierce it made him shake.

As he settled onto a bunk below, anticipating a nice, long nap, he had a premonition of trouble. Just a twinge though; not enough to keep him awake. He shook it off, sighed deeply, and closed his eyes.

As he slept soundly, God blew a fierce storm in and over the ship with a fury of epic proportions. The ship was catapulted up one wave and tossed down another, all the while taking on water faster than the crew could bail it out. In abject fear, the men threw out everything they could get their hands on to lighten the boat, but to no avail.

They were going down – they knew it. Prayers were lifted and last confessions made.

Then one of the sailors got the bright idea to cast lots to see whose bad behavior was causing all this trouble.

Hah! They knew it – Jonah!

They sent someone down to wake him up. The burly crewman grabbed Jonah by the scruff of the neck and virtually dragged him up the steps, unceremoniously tossing him to the deck.

Every sailor surrounded Jonah, leaned in close, and raised their voices to be heard over the scream of the storm. Their eyes were bright with fear as they interrogated him. Jonah told them all the truth. He tried to stand up straight and tall, but the heaving of the ship made it impossible, or was it his own inner wretchedness?

Jonah knew why the storm had blown up so quickly. So, because he did care about the lives of the ship's crew, he told them how to make the storm cease. "Toss me into the sea," he said.

Because Jonah would rather die by drowning than go talk to those awful Ninevites; he truly hated them.

In desperation, they reluctantly picked him up and threw him into the sea, begging forgiveness from God as they did so.

The water hit him like a thousand slaps, and the waves pushed him under. Every time he fought his way to the surface, he grabbed a lungful of air, and down he would go again. His limbs grew tired, and as he finally decided to just let himself be carried along, he sank lower and lower, and deeper and deeper, into that murky, swirling chaos called a sea.

His body came to rest on its floor amid the rocks and empty crustacean shells. Seaweed would be his last bed.

A large shadow blocked out the remainder of any natural light, and then he found himself being picked up – well more like sucked in – and the next thing he knew he was slithering down into the stomach of something truly big and nasty.

He gagged and choked on dirty seawater. He could breathe again, but oh, how it stank! And it was slimy and darker than any moonless night he'd ever experienced; not the slightest pinpoint of light to give any sort of comfort.

Could it get any worse?

Jonah knew throwing himself a pity party now wouldn't work so well. So, he did what anyone in his position would do.

He prayed, earnestly and with conviction.

And Jonah got a free ride to Nineveh.

This story ends on a strange note. Nineveh is preached to by a man who is their sworn enemy and they repent of their evil ways. God relents and doesn't destroy them. And Jonah is angry – again.

"Isn't this what I said when I was in my own country?" Jonah remonstrated with God. "You are a God full of mercy."

I've always thought this story ended before it was resolved. You know, the happy ending, the protagonist growing and becoming a better person, learning a valuable lesson; the character arc.

But in this one, the protagonist appears to remain stuck with his angry and unforgiving spirit.

So, God used Jonah – a man who hated those he was preaching to. He used Jonah to bring forgiveness and restoration to a wicked group of people. And at the end of the story, it appears that Jonah still hated them. Why didn't God use another prophet? Why use Jonah at all? God could have given speech to the fish for that matter, like he did to Balaam's donkey.

But no – God chose to use Jonah.

Maybe this is to tell us something.

But what?

I've heard people say "I just can't forgive them" – I've said those words myself before. But that's not true. We choose. We either choose to forgive or we choose to hold tightly to our anger and hate.

I know – when you've been hurt so deeply, it can feel like you can't. Forgiveness can be a process, not necessarily a once-and-done.

God expects our cooperation and obedience. But He doesn't need those things to accomplish His purposes. He prefers them, but He doesn't need them.

We can choose to stumble through life fighting against the hand holding ours, as toddlers do when they don't want to go where their parents are taking them. We can fight against Him. We will lose. And He will win. Always.

He will get the things done He wants done – with or without an agreeable attitude on our part.

Our life isn't about us. Ever.

It's always, always, always about Him.

And when we dispatch our duties with servants' hearts, we will not only grow; we'll become more usable. But know this - His purposes will happen no matter what.

I'd like to think Jonah, as he walked away from Nineveh in disgust, finished with his task and tired of waiting to see if they'd burn, began to get a glimpse of this truth. And that by the time he arrived back home, he himself repented.

Jonah was not a reluctant prophet; he was a stiff-necked and angry prophet who God chose to use anyway.

We don't hear anything more about Jonah. We don't know if God ever used him to deliver a message again.

This story always makes me think of that passage of Scripture, *"don't grieve the Holy Spirit."(Ephesians 4:30)* Don't you think God was deeply grieved by Jonah's attitude?

My anger finally ran its course and my depression lifted. God was patient with me while I worked through all the emotions that threatened to drown me: my accusing words, my raised fist, and my closed-up heart. He still used me through this process to share the good news, even while I was immersed in my own disappointment and pain. Even as I clung to His promises with my last strength, as a climber grasps the crumbling rocks with shaking fingers, feet desperately and blindly searching for a foothold.

This chapter is especially for you who are struggling today with anger, hopelessness, and disappointment. Yes, God's desire is for us to rest, trust, and be filled with joy. But He also knows us intimately and loves us through our mess. Hang in there and crawl if you can't walk. Be better than Jonah – choose forgiveness and allow it to do its work and grace to fill your eyes, so that love is what you're able to give.

Just like Jesus said, *"It is not the healthy who need a doctor, but the sick." (Mark 2:17)*

Let His healing hands begin the healing process for you today.

Chapter 6

Jaw-Cracking and Peace-Making

Our Belgians' hooves kicked up miniature dust clouds as they walked in the corral. These were sorrel-colored work horses the size of Clydesdales, but without the "feathers." The warm, summer day was bright and windless. I was working in the stuffy barn, perspiration stinging my eyes, mucking out the stalls surrounded by the sweet smell of alfalfa hay and the pungent odor of horse manure. One of our barn cats was nursing her newest litter of mewling kittens on a pile of fresh straw, their tiny paws kneading her sides as they filled their bellies. Dale, a gelding, our mare Katie, and her new foal, Kip, were outside in the fenced corral attached to the barn, stretching their legs; their tails constantly flicking flies from their sweat-shined coats.

Kip was a brand-new foal of just a few days. I had watched his birth, commiserating with Katie during her labor, for I was acquainted with that kind of pain. I could see it in her eyes. At Katie's final push, Kip slid out still encased in his amniotic sac and as soon as his tightly curled-up body touched the dusty ground, the sac split neatly from his head to his hooves. His chest heaved, he opened his eyes, and struggled to stand, all wobbly on his knobby knees; his legs trembling, breathing deeply of the life-giving air.

After just a few days, he was trotting around outside with his momma, growing stronger every day. After taking care of my chores in the barn, I walked outside and witnessed a sight I'll never forget.

Dale was bullying Kip and had just nipped him. As I exited the barn, I saw Kip attempting to get away from the much bigger horse. It seemed only a fraction of a second. Suddenly Katie was there in all her motherly indignation, whinnying, forcing Dale into a corner of the corral. Katie ran circles around him, making terrifying noises, while the dusty earth boiled up around them both like smoke from a furnace. She got him cornered, his rear to the rails, turned her back to him and swiftly kicked him in the jaw with both back legs twice, in succession, with lighting speed and deadly accuracy. A horrific crack reverberated in the air, then she calmly trotted off to join her baby.

Dale stood there for a long time, his head hanging down; clearly in a lot of pain and embarrassment in his very stance.

This scene of maternal protectiveness scored itself deeply into my memory. Kip stood safely off to the side while his momma kicked butt, or jaw as was the case. She did what it took to protect her baby. Dale never bullied Kip again.

The picture of boiling dust, a screaming horse, and justice swiftly served was how I viewed my periodic times of conflict. I was Katie, delivering justice. But for me, I wasn't protecting anyone but myself. I had felt alone for most of my life and the only one sticking up for me was me. It was a lonely feeling.

I had something happen recently to put a new spin on this for me. It seems I've been meting out justice for myself unnecessarily. I had the picture all wrong. I wasn't Katie; I was Kip. And God was telling me through the wise counsel of my older son that He would be doing any kicking needed this time.

Have you been taken advantage of? Lied about and lied to? Expected to "take it" and go along to get along? It sticks in your craw, doesn't it? My fighting instincts take over, and I'm ready to kick them in the jaw and make them behave. Some things in life are black and white, right or wrong.

My prickly personality comes out in earnest, as I feel I'm fighting for my life. I don't back down and I don't give in. However.

"A person's wisdom yields patience; It is to one's glory to overlook an offense." (Proverbs 19:11)

Jeremy reminded me that my job is to be salt and light, not make sure I'm always treated with the respect I deserve. Learning how to defuse a situation and speak words of edification coupled with compassion is needed to live the life God desires of us.

Remember the fruits of the Spirit? It's not always convenient to think about them, is it? *"But the fruit of the Spirit is love, joy, peace, patience, kindness, goodness, gentleness, self-control; against such things there is no law." (Galatians 5:22-23, ESV)*

I love the opening paragraph in the preface of Ken Sande's book *The Peacemaker*. "Peacemakers are people who breathe grace. They draw continually on the goodness and power of Jesus Christ, and then they bring his love, mercy, forgiveness, strength, and wisdom to the conflicts of daily life." (Sande, 2004).

There's a fine line between enabling bad behavior, because I've certainly been there, done that, and stepping back and allowing God to use you to handle a situation with eternity in mind. That may mean submitting under God to be taken advantage of. What's the difference, you're wondering?

That's an excellent question and I'm not sure I have a clear answer. I think motivation has a lot to do with it. What is my motivation for cracking someone's jaw? What is the bigger picture? Who is watching this all play out? Will Christ be honored by my behavior? Will a weaker brother or sister, or an unbeliever, be hurt by how I handle this?

These are important questions, and wisdom is called for.

I need to breathe grace.

I stepped back, did a lot of praying, and responded calmly and without anger. I felt I needed them to at least understand my point of view, remembering to attack the problem, not the person; trying to find a win/win so everyone can walk away happy with the outcome. And now, I leave the decision to God.

In the past, Katie would come out in me. The dust would rise like smoke from my harsh words as I pushed with them, choosing each word carefully like David did the stones he placed in his sling; verbally shoving them against a wall until I got what I wanted, without regard to any damage being done to the relationship.

But that's not the way Jesus wants me to be. I encourage you to take the time to slowly and prayerfully read Matthew chapter 5 and tell me I was right in going on the attack. Tough words to read, aren't they?

"Blessed are the merciful, for they shall be shown mercy." (v. 7)

"Blessed are the peacemakers, for they will be called children of God." (v. 9)

"You are the salt of the earth. But if the salt loses its saltiness, how can it be made salty again?" (v. 13)

"You have heard that it was said, 'Eye for eye, and tooth for tooth.' But I tell you, do not resist an evil person. If anyone slaps you on the right cheek, turn to them the other cheek also. And if anyone wants to sue you and take your shirt, hand over your coat as well. If anyone forces you to go one mile, go with them two miles." (v. 38-41)

My testimony must remain intact. My motivation must be pure. Remember I've said before that our time here is to train us for eternity?

Hebrews chapter 12 is a powerful exhortation on how we should conduct ourselves. Here's just a few verses:

> *Consider him who endured from sinners such hostility against himself, so that you may not grow weary or fainthearted. In your struggle against sin you have not yet resisted to the point of shedding your blood. And have you forgotten the exhortation that addressed you as sons? "My son, do not regard lightly the discipline of the Lord, nor be weary when reproved by him. For the Lord disciplines the one he loves and chastises every son whom he receives." It is for discipline that you have to endure. God is treating you as sons. (Hebrews 12:3-7, ESV)*

Being a child of the Most High God is an awesome, incomparable privilege and I am

Jaw-Cracking and Peace-Making

thankful for human angels God has placed in my life to remind me of whose I am and the important work I need to be about.

Stay focused on eternity. Work on resolving conflict with patience and compassion. If there's to be any jaw-kicking, let your heavenly Father take care of it.

Strive to be known as a peacemaker who breathes grace.

Section Three

SERVING

Wings

The time I've spent;
The words I've used
Were all for you,
Were all for you.

I watched and waited for my star to rise.
I searched the horizon long.
My ship, it hasn't come.

Did I not wait long enough?
Was I not good at scanning the distant shore?
Where did I fail you?

An unfinished symphony, it's said, is life.
My heart aches to hear the chorus.
My ears strain to catch the melody.

Did I make too many mistakes?
Did you get tired of waiting for me?
Have you set me aside, unused and forgotten?

Through Cracked Glass

Then why have I felt a stirring in my heart of late,
A restlessness of spirit;
A deep desire to stretch my wings and fly.

But where are my wings?
I don't see them.
I don't see them.
But I want to fly!

I walk through my days unseen, it seems.
Unknown;
Just one of many.
No one special.
No one with something extraordinary to give.
Won't someone see in my eyes
That I can be,
I can do
So much more,
So much more?

But you must see me.
How can I make you see me?
Won't someone see me?

What is this sprouting from my back?
Can they be the wings I've longed for?
When shall I fly?
Where shall I fly?

Command me and I'll go.
Speak the words and I'm there.
Spirit me away to new places,
New hearts,
Open hearts.

I awake.
Where have you sent me?
Let my burning heart proclaim,
To all who will hear
Words of life,
Words of love,
Words of peace.

Ow! Something hurts.
My wings, they bleed,
But they still carry me.
All I ask is that they still carry me.
I can endure the pain.
I see the distant horizon.

Send me again.

To serve my King
Is all I desire.
My heart is full,
Overflowing.
Let me burn out for you.

Thank you for my wings.

Helping, Serving, Healing

The whole concept of helping others, serving others, and healing others grew in me as a seed is placed in humus-rich soil and begins pushing out roots, growing toward the sun.

As you can no doubt tell from previous chapters, I, unfortunately, hadn't given this important facet of life a place of prominence in my day-to-day journey. It was hardly on my radar for many years.

I focused on raising my children and running a household. I homeschooled them and, since we lived out in the country, always had a large garden to plant and harvest, chickens to tend to, and horses to curry. We did sponsor children from Compassion, and after more than twenty years, I still have a child I sponsor whose name is Kim, from the Philippines. I think I've sponsored about six different children over the years. It's a wonderful organization doing God's work.

The real transformation began back, again, in Arizona. Through those three books I mentioned before (*A Million Miles in a Thousand Years,* by Don Miller, *Outlive Your Life,* by Max Lucado, and *The Walk,* by Richard Paul Evans), God opened for me a desire to be used for something – I suddenly wanted to be remembered for a legacy of service to others; not how much money I'd earned or how big my house was or how nice my things were.

You must remember, I'm an introvert and being alone is what I prefer most of the time. Serving others meant I'd have to interact with people and open myself up to feeling their pain, and possibly not maintaining that so-carefully-groomed emotional control. Life was going to get much more complicated.

I also consumed other books with similar ideas. Books like *Radical* by David Platt and *Love Does,* Bob Goff's first book, and a book I've been quoting from, Brennan Manning's *The Furious Longing of God.* As I read and meditated on them, along with the Scriptures,

I was astounded at what I had been missing out on all these years.

While living in Arizona, I became involved with Operation Christmas Child, a branch of Samaritan's Purse run by Franklin Graham, and enjoyed the opportunity to be part of such a Christ-centered organization helping children around the world. Franklin's book *Rebel With a Cause* helped cement in me the importance of what our real purposes here are.

Once I moved back to Michigan, I was spending most of my time serving my parents, but once I landed a part-time retail job, so I could continue to make my car payments, I was able to find ways to plant seeds of the gospel there as I interacted with customers. Sometimes I would have only a minute or two, but I planted the seeds anyway and prayed that God would bring the increase.

Things really gained momentum when God moved me to Florida and I found myself attending Northstar Church, an imperfect group of believers whose focus is "helping the whole world find and follow Jesus." They are dead serious about serving their community, and I've learned a lot about selflessness and sacrifice during my sojourn here. Their constant example of self-giving has been inspiring.

Something else that changed how I see others happened when my son was sentenced to prison. I was suddenly forced to look at and interact with other prisoners when I'd go and visit my son every Saturday. The Spirit was whispering to my heart – "I see value in them. Look at them with my eyes."

These two settings, becoming part of a local church who loves its community and seeing prisoners from God's perspective, effectively adjusted how I view the world. We are all broken, and we are all loved by God who sent Jesus to die for not just those of us who are only kind-of bad, but for the incorrigibly bad. The apostle John meant it when he penned these words that most of us know by heart: *"For God so loved the world that he gave his one and only Son, that whoever believes in him shall not perish but have eternal life"* *(John 3:16).*

He didn't say, "For God so loved the good people and the pretty good people and the people who keep their nose clean." He said the world, and that includes a whole host of goodness and badness.

So, you see, these were lessons I couldn't learn in Arizona. I had to learn them in Florida — the perfect environment. I was drafted for a lead part in an epic drama and given my lines. I had to practice them over and over and become the character so that in the end the lines weren't delivered by an actor, but by a true believer.

These next stories span many years. As I looked back on my life, there were things that happened I didn't fully understand at the time, but now am able to clearly see the lesson behind the scene.

I'd like to end this introduction with a lengthy passage from, once again, Brennan Manning's masterpiece, *The Furious Longing of God:*

> Healing is a response to a crisis in the life of another person. It's enough of a response, a satisfactory response to a crisis in the

life of another. And wherever the word *crisis* is used in the Greek New Testament, it is translated in English as *judgment.* That's right – *judgment.* Healing is a response that I make to a decisive moment in the life of a brother or sister; whether I respond or not, I have made a judgment.

Healing becomes the opportunity to pass off to another human being what I have received from the Lord Jesus; namely His unconditional acceptance of me as I am, not as I should be. He loves me whether in a state of grace or disgrace, whether I live up to the lofty expectations of His gospel or I don't. He comes to me where I live and loves me as I am.

When I have passed that same reality on to another human being, the result most often has been the inner healing of their heart through the touch of my affirmation. To affirm a person is to see good in them that they cannot see in themselves and to repeat it in spite of appearances to the contrary. Please, this is not a Pollyanna optimism that is blind to the reality of evil, but rather like a fine radar system that is tuned in to the true, the good, and the beautiful. When a person is evoked for who she is, not who she is not, the most often result will be the inner healing of her heart through the touch of affirmation. (Manning, 2009)

Chapter 1

Momma

I feel like I've spent too much space venting about my momma, and it's time I say some nice things about her, because she was nice.

As I mentioned before, she was a wonderful southern cook. She made the best green beans I've ever eaten. Over the years, I've tried again and again to copy her recipe, to no avail. Mine never taste the same. And her mashed potatoes were fabulous – the only thing I was able to do better than her. Then there were her baking powder biscuits to die for, fluffy and perfectly browned.

When I was young, she sang alto in a quartet at the small church we attended. She told me one day that her daddy, my Papaw, used to sing in a quartet and even traveled to different churches to sing. I learned how to sing harmony from her. She played records by Conway

Twitty and Loretta Lynn and taught me how to sing along with them. To this day, I have a hard time singing the melody on a song, because my voice, after so many decades of practice, naturally finds the harmony. Every time I am privileged to sing in our praise band at church, I thank my momma.

Once my older brother, sister, and myself were grown and out of the household, and my youngest brother was in high school, she took up housecleaning to bring in extra spending money and for something to do since it was hard for her to sit still. She cleaned other people's houses and when she was done, it was clean. You might have thought it was clean before she showed up, but once she had touched things, they shone. You could always tell when Momma had cleaned. It was a gift. She took her time, doing as thorough a job as anyone I've ever seen.

She also had a generous heart and would give you the shirt off her back. I remember when I was first married, and still a naïve, inexperienced bride of nineteen, she would show up at our little apartment with bags of groceries. She always brought some of my favorite food. She didn't know how to say "I love you" in so many words, but she said it with what she brought. It was torture for her to let go of control, so buying food and delivering it to my door was her next best thing. She never really liked her first son-in-law.

Watching her feed people when they came over (which wasn't often until my kids became teenagers and they brought their friends) to the house showed me something. Seeing her force someone to take money or a trinket or clothing she'd bought for them showed me something too.

For all her crazy issues, she cared about others as best she could. And I have learned to appreciate and emulate her generosity.

So even though I didn't really focus on serving others until I was much older, looking back at how my mom used her spiritual gift has given me encouragement.

Because of my sister's many mental issues, she lived in a group home from the time she was about nineteen until she died a few years ago. Before she became sick, Mom visited my sister regularly, and she always brought groceries for her, even though the group home fed the residents. Their food wasn't quite good enough and asking for things was my sister's way of getting attention from Mom. And Momma got to know some of the residents when she'd visit with my sister, so it became common for her to bring presents for some of the other mentally ill, but still precious, souls who called that place home. If she made up her mind to like you, she had the capacity to shower you with gifts. It made her immensely happy.

So, I came by my desire to serve others legitimately, as the saying goes. I learned it from my momma.

I learned that God can use us in the middle of our messes and failings. I learned that even when our lives are disasters and our hearts are struggling with other issues, God will still cause our plants to bloom for Him and bear fruit.

"And if you spend yourselves on behalf of the hungry and satisfy the needs of the oppressed, then your light will rise in the darkness, and your night will become like the noonday." (Isaiah 58:10)

Chapter 2

Dad

It occurred to me that at this point I've not talked a lot about my dad. I'm a committed daddy's girl, so it's hard for me to see any wrong in him. I know it's there, of course. But I look at him, like many daughters, through rose-colored glasses, always believing the best.

Which, by the way, is how God wants us to love others.

This portion of my memoir is about serving, and I believe my dad served his family by remaining steadfast and faithful. We weren't rich by any standard of measure, but we never lacked either. We had everything we needed. He was, and still is, a hard worker.

His true test of serving came during Momma's illness and physical decline. I had fully expected to live there with my parents for the long haul, but, as you already know, after about two years of being Momma's co-caregiver, God moved me to Florida.

I felt guilty leaving them. Momma cried, begging me to stay. I remember her standing in front of me, with tears running down her face. "I need you!" Her little girl voice drove the stake of guilt deeper into my heart. It was so difficult, on one hand, to leave. On the other hand, it was a relief of sorts, because Momma had, by that time, gotten quite difficult to care for. Her mood swings were greater and greater, and many days I felt we were at loggerheads. Discord and frustration filled too much of the day, and it was affecting Dad's ability to care for her. I had served them for two years, teaching Dad how to cook, do laundry, and clean, and encouraged him as best I could. It was time for me to move on.

My maternal instinct had taken over when my son was convicted and sentenced. I had a good reason to move away, but the guilt remained. My younger brother, by that time, had moved in with Mom and Dad, so I knew they'd have some additional assistance.

The constant strain on Dad was at times overwhelming. He confided in me about how her illness affected him. My oldest daughter, Rachael, was able, for a few months, to stop in a couple times a week to visit with Momma and give Dad a break. Momma enjoyed Rachael's company and it warmed my heart seeing my daughter loving her Mamaw like she did. The last year of Momma's life, Dad brought in a licensed professional so he could get a few hours of respite several days a week. It gave him the opportunity to run errands or just work in his pole barn or mow the grass without wondering what Momma was getting into.

He kept her at home for as long as he could. For the last eight months or so of her life, she had deteriorated to the point where she was constantly trying to "escape." She'd take off down the street or walk up to a neighbor's house and knock on their door, begging for help. Dad would have to track her down, explain to the neighbors what was really going on, and try to convince her to come back home. Remaining the incorrigible person she had always been, this stage of her disease was especially problematic. He finally had to place her in a facility. It was the most difficult decision he'd ever had to make. By that time, Momma's world had shrunk to almost nothing. She knew no one and feared everything. She cried when you washed her hair or bathed her. She'd cry for no reason at all, sobbing uncontrollably while Dad held her, attempting to soothe her unknown fears. I was concerned I'd lose both.

She only lived for a few weeks after being placed in a facility just a few miles from their home. Momma, stubborn to the last, refused to accept the change. But I can understand why she finally gave up. She had had enough. Her entire world had vanished. She was a stranger to herself.

"...for richer, for poorer, in sickness, and in health..."

Dad cared for Momma as the dementia robbed her slowly and irrevocably of her own personhood. His stress was my stress and his heartaches were my heartaches. I watched him take it on the chin more times than I can count. His patience and longsuffering with her were testaments to me of what serving another truly means.

The last time I saw Momma was in June when I flew there for a short visit. I knew she wouldn't be with us much longer. Dad was so exhausted and emotionally drained, and Momma was hateful and spiteful. I remember she tried to get out of the house – she kept saying she wanted to live somewhere else – and I had to block the doorway to keep her from opening the door. She picked something up and threw it at me. She hated Dad but, at the same time, didn't want him out of her sight. The year before, when my sister died, she accused him of causing her death and ripped all the beautiful flowers apart that kind friends had bought for the funeral. I know it was her way of attempting to deal with the grief. But the hurt in Dad's eyes was almost more than I could stand.

But he never lashed out; he knew she wasn't in control anymore. He understood and hung in there, no matter what she did or what she said. Did he do it perfectly? Of course not. But his patience and gentleness were the norm. He exercised a measure of self-control that is not often seen anymore.

In the end, the words perseverance, gentleness, and kindness – those fruits of the Spirit Paul speaks about in Galatians – were made real to me as I watched true love in action during the worst of times.

> *Love is patient, love is kind. It does not envy, it does not boast, it is not proud. It does not dishonor others, it is not self-seeking, it is not easily angered, it keeps no record of wrongs. Love does not delight in evil but rejoices with the truth. It always protects, always trusts, always hopes, always perseveres." (1 Corinthians 13:4-7)*

I strive to be as good at serving as my parents were. It's a tough act to follow, but I'm not giving up.

Chapter 3

Billy-Bob

The day had grown warm and sunny on that end-of-spring, beginning-of-summer day in Michigan so many years ago, and I was getting a bit of fresh air outside in the yard. My first husband and I had bought a small, what I called "farm-ette," a few years before out in the country with about fifty-five acres of land. We put in a large garden every year, had laying hens for fresh eggs, too many barn cats, one dog, and several Belgian work horses. The front twenty-five or so acres were tillable land, and the back acreage was wooded and filled with squirrels, chipmunks, opossums, deer, and the occasional skunk.

In the yard, I had perennials beginning to bloom, and lilacs sharing their heady scent. Over by our recently painted barn, I was stepping across a water puddle left over from the previous day's rain when I noticed a small, dead, naked baby bird lying, discarded, in the cold water.

Poor little thing! I thought. I sighed deeply and looked upward, instinctively, to see if I could determine from where he had fallen, but the tree was too leafed out and the branches too high for me to locate his nest. My youngest daughter Bethany, about eight years old at the time, loved all things nature, and because I was homeschooling my children, I decided this tiny bird with the translucent skin would be a great science lesson. You could see all the little guy's organs through his delicate, perfectly formed, and featherless body.

I carefully carried his little ice-cold body (because I had already decided this little bird was male) into the house, cupped in my hand to show my daughter.

Her beautiful, big eyes grew even bigger when she recognized what I had in my hand. She brushed her silky hair from her face. "See, sweetie, how you can see all his little organs. Isn't it amazing how God puts us together?"

"Is he dead, Momma?" her little child voice asked me, with a quaver, getting right to what she saw as the real point. She started to reach out her finger to touch him, then pulled back.

"I'm afraid so. He must have fallen out of his nest. I found him in the water puddle outside near the barn."

She looked so sad, and his body was so cold. I began to softly stroke him to warm him up. Suddenly, he convulsed, crapped out a load, and opened his eyes.

I'm sure both our jaws hit the floor in complete and utter surprise. Then we laughed uproariously.

Our family already had an African Grey parrot we had raised from a baby, because the kids' dad had always wanted a bird he could train to talk; and I still had some of the powdered bird food left over in the pantry. I rummaged around and located it, along with an eye-dropper, mixed some of the powder with water, then, with Bethany's assistance, used the eye-dropper to get some food into our new, little, never-say-die family member.

We decided to call him Billy-Bob.

Bethany and I poked around in the closets, finally locating a small, abandoned aquarium that had previously housed a hamster (who was now buried in the backyard), cleaned it up, put some soft rags inside, and gently placed little Billy-Bob in, once we had him fed.

He was a voracious eater, letting me know with squeaky chirping when he was hungry, which turned out to be quite frequently.

After a couple of weeks, he was strong enough and feathered out enough to stand on a perch in a previously unused bird cage. For some reason, he always looked like he was frowning.

By then, he had graduated from an eyedropper to eating his food mixture out of a spoon. He was small but tough and I loved him. After a few more weeks, I took him outside – he would sit on my finger – and let him fly off. He flew to one of our trees, perched himself on a high branch, and proceeded to call to me in his own language. I kept telling him I couldn't reach him up there, but he continued to chirp.

After a short while, I went inside, mixed some of his food, brought it back outside, and tapped the spoon on the side of the small, plastic cup containing his supper. The tapping sound was something he recognized, and he flew down out of the tree and perched on my finger like always.

We played this little game for another week or so, until he didn't come back. In the meantime, in anticipation of this event, I had installed a bird feeder in the backyard, where I would watch Billy-Bob and many other birds come to eat out of it with my binoculars for the rest of that summer.

You're wondering how I recognized him? One of his tail feathers was crooked, so I could always tell my Billy-Bob apart from the other birds.

I'll bet you're also wondering what kind of bird Billy-Bob was. He was just a common sparrow. Nothing special, except to us.

We lavished our love and attention on this most common and insignificant of all birds.

I've always believed life is a series of lessons preparing us for eternity. And each lesson, no matter how insignificant it may seem, teaches us important truths we need to master. And each encounter, no matter how small, causes ripples through the fabric of time that, someday, we'll know where and how far they went.

So, until we know the end of the story, let's make sure God can use us to bring life back from the dead, and healing and health to those who seem to be without hope. If you stay alert, I guarantee you'll find common sparrows in the cold puddles of life needing the warmth of your touch.

Be the one God uses to bring another Billy-Bob back from the dead.

> ..."And who is my neighbor?" In reply Jesus said: "A man was going down from Jerusalem to Jericho, when he fell into the hands of robbers. They stripped him of his clothes, beat him and went away, leaving him half dead. A priest happened to be going down the same road, and

when he saw the man, he passed by on the other side. So, too, a Levite, when he came to the place and saw him, passed by on the other side. But a Samaritan, as he traveled, came where the man was; and when he saw him, he took pity on him. He went to him and bandaged his wounds, pouring on oil and wine. Then he put the man on his own donkey, took him to an inn and took care of him. The next day he took out two silver coins and gave them to the innkeeper. 'Look after him,' he said, 'and when I return, I will reimburse you for any extra expense you may have.' 'Which of these three do you think was a neighbor to the man who fell into the hands of robbers?" The expert in the law replied, "The one who had mercy on him." Jesus told him, "Go, and do likewise."'" (Luke 10:29-37)

Chapter 4

Finding Our Way Back Home

The November temperature was dropping below freezing, with the sun now below the horizon and full dark fast approaching. And my ten-year-old son Jeremy and I had lost the blood trail.

We'd been following the spoor for the last half hour or so, but now it was too dark to see any more blood drops on the forest floor.

It wasn't my first year hunting, but it was my first and only year bow-hunting on our land in Michigan, because the deer I had hit with my arrow hadn't dropped as expected. The seven-point buck bolted through the trees and we couldn't find him anywhere. I used the venison every winter to feed my family, but bow-hunting was clearly not working for me. My shotgun was much more effective. My purpose in hunting wasn't to injure and maim, but to kill instantly with minimal, if any, suffering. You may think this is silly, but I always thanked the deer for helping me feed my family.

We had about twenty-five acres of woods at the back of our property, with the front thirty acres or so tillable land. This past year it had been alfalfa, and the year before the field had been full of row upon row of corn. One year we tried putting in oats, but that year we had a drought so there was no crop to harvest. We lived in a rural area where most of the houses had significant amounts of acreage attached. Because of the various crops grown in the area, and creeks and streams close by, there were some large deer herds living in the woods. Sometimes, a farmer would kick up some deer while tilling his fields. In the winter, if the snows were significant and lasted well into the spring, some of the deer would die of starvation if they were unable to find vegetation under the snow.

I'm not all that good navigating in the woods, even though I love being in it. I can get turned around too easily, so after the buck ran off through the trees with my arrow still in him, I made my way back to the house and asked Jeremy if he'd like to help me track the deer I'd shot.

"Sure, Mom, I'll help you." He donned his heavy coat, hat, scarf, gloves, and waterproof boots, then followed me out the door, walked the eighth of a mile up the two-track lane with me, and into the woods as the sun sank even lower in the sky and the colors, almost like blood, streaked across the horizon.

It was a noisy walk, because there wasn't any snow on the ground yet, just dead and very crackly leaves, alerting every critter around of our presence even though we did our best to be quiet. We carefully tracked the blood drops for as long as we could.

When it was finally too dark to see, and time to head home to try again tomorrow, I looked up to the sky to get my bearings. I did a complete circle searching for a familiar tree line outlined against the starry sky, and then my old friend fear gripped me and my heart began beating too hard in my chest. Panic was right there and, as I willed myself to calm down, I said to my son with a wobble in my voice, "I'm a little turned around; do you know exactly where we are?"

"Of course I do, Mom!" my confident ten-year-old said, with a smile in his little-boy voice. "Here, take my hand and follow me, I'll lead us home."

So, I did, and soon we were out of the woods, standing in the field, gazing at the welcoming lights of home just down the lane.

I've had to overcome a lot of things over the years that used to terrify me. I'll bet you have too. One of my biggies, though, if you permit me to admit it, is allowing myself to be vulnerable to the hurts of others. It's easier for me to give money, give things, and pray for someone than to drive to their house, or call them on the phone, sit down face to face, eye to eye, voice to voice, and gaze on their private wounds and trace their scars.

Because, if you're like me, you feel inadequate and uncomfortable in situations like that. There's just too much emotion going on. I don't know what to say or how to fix the issue. People and their problems are a messy business, and it drains me dry emotionally. I absorb too much and feel too much, and it scares me because then I'm not in control anymore.

When I start thinking thoughts like that, though, I remember this saying by an unknown author: "God doesn't call the equipped, He equips the called." And, what God said to the apostle Paul – *"My strength is made perfect in weakness." (II Corinthians 12:9)*

Our meager, emotional resources are more than enough for God to use. Just as He fed five thousand hungry people with only five loaves of bread and two small fish, He can use you and me, especially when we feel inadequate.

Jeremy had no idea how much his young voice and mittened hand calmed his momma's fears. He didn't know a lot of things – he was just a little boy. But he knew how to get us back home.

People who are hurting are just looking for someone to show them the way home; the way out of their pain and back to the comforting lights just down the lane.

"Not all of us can do great things. But we can do small things with great love." Mother Teresa

Chapter 5

A LITTLE LAMB

My feet were beginning to hurt like they tended to do after a few hours into my shift. But that's retail work for you. There's not any sitting down happening unless you're on your scheduled 15-minute break or your 30-minute timed lunch.

But it was a sunny day, which always made me more cheerful, and they had put me on the self-scans, where I preferred to be. But I guess I should back up just a bit.

The previous year, I had packed up my Chevy Malibu and driven across the country from Arizona to Michigan, after resigning from my good-paying job and emptying out my condo. As you know from previous chapters, my mom had been diagnosed with dementia/Alzheimer's, and I knew Dad would be needing some help. We had decided to keep Mom at home for as long as possible, so I moved in and assisted where I could. But I still had a car payment to make, so I also had to find some part-time work, and retail was about the extent of what I could locate. The pay was super low, but it was better than nothing.

I enjoyed working the self-scans because it was fast-paced, and it gave me the opportunity to interact with tons of people for just a few minutes at a time. I guess it was a little like speed dating. I enjoyed keeping my area neat and tidy, and the equipment clean and in good working order. It's funny how such simple things can bring us pleasure.

There were some fascinating personalities that would come into the store and it was a fun diversion to be able to interact with them, if only for a couple of minutes. A few wooden benches had been placed across the wall at the front of the store, and it was common to see some of our elderly patrons sitting there for an hour or more waiting for, usually a wife, to complete her shopping. I remember one time a gentleman had been sitting there for an extended wait, and I became a little concerned. I went over to him and jokingly asked if he needed me to contact DFS (Department of Family Services) on his behalf. We both had a good laugh. Just about that time, his wife walked up to the check-out with a cart loaded with all kinds of things she'd found.

There was another elderly gentleman who would come to the store every week. He could barely walk, shuffling slowly down the aisle. He had had some surgery on his foot, so we would cheer him on as he did some of his physical therapy right there in the store, and he would give us a huge smile, as we clapped for him. One day, I noticed his shoelace was untied, so I ran up to him, put my hand on his shoulder to get his attention, then knelt down and tied his shoe.

On one afternoon there was a lull in the busyness, and a middle-aged woman walked up and began scanning the items in her cart. She picked one item up, looked at it pensively, and started to put it off to the side. She glanced up and saw me watching her.

"Is it ok for me to put this down if I've decided I don't want it?" she asked.

"Sure, but I can take it for you. It's not a problem." I walked up to her and accepted the small, stuffed lamb she held out to me. It was on clearance for $5.99. "This is so adorable!" I exclaimed. "If you don't want it, I just might buy it myself." I pressed the sticker over the little lamb's heart, and it began to sing that old Sunday School song, *Jesus loves me*.

Jesus loves me, this I know,
For the Bible tells me so,
Little ones to Him belong,
They are weak but He is strong.

Yes, Jesus loves me,
Yes, Jesus loves me,
Yes, Jesus loves me,
The Bible tells me so.

I looked back at her, and she said, hesitantly, "Can I ask you a question? I need your opinion on something."

"Of course!" I replied.

"I was going to get it for my daughter's best friend, but I'm afraid she's too old and might think a stuffed animal is for babies."

"Why, how old is she?" I asked.

"She's nineteen, and in the hospital dying. The doctor says she has only about a week to live and I wanted to get her something, but I just don't know if this would be good or not." I could hear the sadness in her voice, with tears just below the surface.

"You know, I think one of the best things to bring comfort and peace when you're dying would be something like this. You're never too old to hear that Jesus loves you."

As the lady took the lamb back from me and purchased it, and walked out the door, I took a moment to say a prayer for that nineteen-year-old girl whose life was ending before it had really begun. I prayed that that small, stuffed lamb singing an age-old favorite would bring not only her comfort, but everyone who loved her as well.

When I looked up the author of the song, here's what I found on Wikipedia: "'Jesus Loves Me' is a Christian hymn written by

Anna Bartlett Warner (1827–1915). The lyrics first appeared as a poem in the context of an 1860 novel called Say and Seal, written by her older sister Susan Warner (1819–1885), in which the words were spoken as a comforting poem to a dying child."

Retail might not pay much here on earth, but when you're amassing your treasure in heaven, it doesn't matter what your pay scale is down here. It only matters which hearts you took the time to encourage.

Keep your eyes open and your heart available. You never know who God is going to send to your check-out lane.

Chapter 6

WHEN OUR HEARTS FALL DOWN

I write articles for a couple of the local newspapers in Florida where I live. Some of the articles cover local news, and some are more inspirational in nature. In 2017, when Hurricanes Harvey and Irma devasted Houston and south Florida, I wrote an article about what happened, hoping to bring some measure of comfort and encouragement to my readers.

Then, a year almost to the day later, Hurricane Michael landed, literally, in my backyard and hurt many of my friends. These weren't strangers I watched with compassion on television. No, these were neighbors and friends: my church family, my cashier, my doctor, and my hairstylist. These were hard-working southerners who wanted to live their lives and take care of themselves and their families. It was very up close and personal for me. I wept over so much loss and destruction.

But these resilient people picked themselves up and got to work. The article I had written the year before was still very apropos a year later. I've included it here with permission:

Years ago, I had an elderly friend from Alabama. I grew up in Michigan, so her euphemisms were cute and, usually, right to the point. If I were going to say to you right now, hey, would you like me to tell you about Harvey and Irma and how neighbors helped neighbors and strangers helped strangers?

She would say – "That's what I KNOW!"

So, yeah, that's exactly what you already know.

I've been re-reading one of my favorite books over the past few days. We'll, it's actually two books; the first book followed by the sequel. The first book ends on a heightened note of destruction and despair, leaving you with dropped jaw and tears in your eyes. The second book ends on a note of hope and deliverance, leaving you with that warm, fuzzy feeling. These are the stories I love to read about; stories with, if not a happy ending, one full of hope for the future.

And that's what happened with Harvey and Irma. The hurricanes, after finally blowing themselves out, ended their stories on a note of destruction and despair, and now we're just beginning the sequel that is full of hope and deliverance.

For example, fishing boats with regular guys searching the flooded streets of Houston for the stranded and bedraggled in need of rescuing. First responders driving up and down the streets before the storm, sounding the alarm. Helicopters hovering over flooded houses, lowering life-saving ropes to waiting hands and terrified hearts. Convoys arriving with much needed food and water, blankets and medicine. Everyday people grilling hot-dogs on the side of I-75, handing out the food for free to evacuees heading for safety.

Homes and businesses destroyed, the newly homeless surveying the damage and wondering when, and if, they will ever be whole again.

My Facebook feed was filled with expressions of encouragement, prayers lifted, and offers of help.

And to top it off, today is September 11th. Remembering the day we lost almost 3,000 of our fellow Americans in three terrorist attacks. And on a personal note, yesterday was the first anniversary of my momma's death. We're feeling a little battered and beat-up today, aren't we?

It's raining outside, as I sit at my dining room table typing this article. We could think of the rain as symbolic of the tears cried for the lives and property lost. We could think of it as symbolic of God washing everything clean, like a new start.

One Facebook post I read went something like this: Instead of praying for me, why don't you give me what I need?

Most of the commenters responded with statements like: Yeah, people only pray to make themselves feel better.

Which made me sad, so I responded that, yes, I believe prayer is very powerful, but I also believe that when you see someone in need, you don't need to pray about it, just provide it, which opened a whole discussion about prayer and whether it's effective or not.

Well, I'm not a theologian, so all I could tell them was that I know prayer is powerful because I've experienced God's intervention many times and encouraged them to talk to God themselves.

But you know what? It seemed like I was beating my head against a wall with my words. Tragedy breaks us and re-shapes us. It's up to us to decide what we're being re-shaped into. We can look at coming destruction and pray, or we can shake our fists at God in anger.

One thing is certain, though. The sequels filled with hope and deliverance, overcoming all odds, are the best stories and the ones we remember most, and the ones we re-read, especially when our hearts fall down.

The books I'm re-reading (A Story Like the Wind and A Far Off Place), feature the Bushmen of South Africa, and other tribes of many years ago. The Bushmen have a rich history full of stories, verbally passed down from generation to generation, and their way of speaking is full of beautiful symbolism and imagery. They have a connection with the earth and living things because of their nomad way of life, and they embrace the cycle of life and death. At the end of the first book, Xhabbo, the Bushman friend, was giving comfort to Nonnie, whose father had been brutally killed, along with scores of others.

> "Xhabbo knew that the stars who hide in light as other things hide in darkness were there to see all today. For the stars do fall in this manner when our hearts fall down. The time when the stars also fall down is while the stars feel that our hearts fall over, because those who had been walking upright, leaving their footprints in the sand, have fallen over on to their sides. Therefore, the stars fall down on account of them,

> *knowing the time when men die and that they must, falling, go to tell other people that a bad thing has happened at another place."*
> *(Van Der Post, 1972)*

Even though we can't see the stars for the clouds and rain, God, who made the stars and the clouds and even the hurricanes, sees all and loves us. And I know that He is pleased to see His children being neighbors to those in need, no matter their station in life.

As Jesus said, the second greatest commandment is this – to love your neighbor as yourself." (Matthew 22:39)

The beautiful and uplifting stories being written in the aftermath of Harvey and Irma will be told and re-told for years to come, bringing encouragement and strength to our hearts when they fall down, reminding us that life, though difficult, is full of light and love and hope.

The rebuilding in the Panhandle of Florida is still a long way from completion. We've had many setbacks and disappointments, but our spirit is strong, and we know God is in control of it all.

The tragedy known as Hurricane Michael has brought out the resilient spirit of these southerners, and revealed to many how much love in action resides in the hearts of the residents in the Panhandle.

Chapter 7

COMING ALONGSIDE

Volleyball and racquetball are my games – at least they used to be. Some years ago, I was even on a volleyball team. But I haven't played in a long time, and one Sunday after church we had a picnic and, lo and behold, a volleyball net replete with volleyball players magically appeared!

Things were going well until I jumped up to smack the ball back over the net. Something went terribly wrong, because my wrist immediately reminded me, painfully and agonizingly, of my age and limitations. The dumb thing about this, though, was I kept playing until I hurt my wrist a second time. Yes, I am ashamed to admit it, but it's true. I'd never seen anyone's wrist swell up so quickly and so big. The pain was excruciating and driving back home was an adventure. I borrowed my grandson's wrist brace – he had sprained his wrist just a couple of months earlier – to help give me some relief.

I ended up with a severe sprain and it was days before I could do any typing, which is what I do at work all day, as well as for fun. What a painful injury! I never really noticed how often I use both hands in many of the things I do every day, like putting toothpaste on my toothbrush. I had to lay the tube down across the sink and use my elbow to squeeze the paste out and onto my toothbrush. And then there's getting dressed or chopping vegetables for a salad. Well, actually I couldn't chop any vegetables; or hold a jar and twist off the lid; or hold an umbrella, my car keys, and my coffee while getting out of my car. Or many other things.

You're thinking, ah! I know where she's going with this story – always be thankful. Well, that is very true, we should always be thankful, but that's not the point I'm making.

A few weeks before my mishap (old age, you are a pain!), I had signed up to prepare some food for a men's retreat and realized I now wasn't able to make the dish of lasagna on my own. So, it became a community effort. My grandson chopped the onion for me, and my daughter emptied the pot of boiling water into the sink after the noodles were done. After that, my grandson helped me layer the ingredients, place the lasagna in the oven, take it out of the oven, and place it in the refrigerator in preparation for the next day's journey.

What was usually simple, fun, and downright easy became impossible for me to accomplish on my own. I needed help.

Almost a year ago now, Hurricane Michael roared through the Panhandle of Florida, completely wiping out Mexico Beach and much of Panama City, doing extensive damage to many communities who are now in dire need of help. Homes are gone, along with all the furniture, clothes, and jobs.

There aren't enough empty houses, hotels, and condos to put up the families. There's not enough of anything right now. Some are still living in tents and some are living in their cars. There is so much need it's overwhelming. Churches and organizations have stepped up as well as many individuals have given their time and money. It's a start, for sure.

Just as I was only having some fun playing a game when I became injured, so all these people were living their lives when God sent Michael to create massive devastation. What are we going to do about it?

When you see life smacking someone around, I would encourage you to take a bit of time and find out just what assistance they need and then meet that need to the best of your ability. I inconvenienced my daughter and grandsons. I even inconvenienced the cashier who had to help me get my debit card out of my wallet to pay for my groceries.

Like my sprained wrist, most traumatic situations are temporary. Just be ready to step up and help chop the onions.

Chapter 8

THE UNWORTHY ONES

Having a convict for a relative is not good party conversation. We all know certain types of people we prefer to avoid; some people you just don't want to be associated with. It will ruin your image.

Like the homeless – they make us uncomfortable. If we give them money, what if they spend it on booze or drugs? What if they keep asking for more? When is enough, enough already?

Then there are the needy people. They aren't homeless, but never seem far from it. They're always needing something. We give and give and give.

What about our odd relatives and irritating co-workers?

But someone who's been in jail or prison is another story altogether. And if they're still incarcerated, they don't exist. They're numbers. They're the scum of the earth. They're not worthy of love or consideration. They're bad people who should be punished and never allowed to forget what they did.

Am I right, or am I right?

When Jesus came on the scene over 2,000 years ago, He turned the world upside down.

He looked at people differently, stepped directly into their lives, and changed them for eternity. Back about five years ago, after my son was incarcerated, I wrote some character studies. One was about a very bad man who wasn't even given a name in the Bible, so I gave him one. I call him Darian.

The insufferable days run together. Why is it always dark, or does it just seem so? The chains cut his arms and legs, making them slippery with blood where they dig in deeply, biting through his skin, especially when he struggles against them. But he refuses to feel the pain. He stinks and can't remember the last time he bathed. His animal ferocity is known far and wide, and he relishes the abject fear in the eyes of those unfortunate enough to cross his path.

When did this never-ending nightmare of evil begin? Sometimes, but not often, he's able to reach far back into his hazy mind and remember fragments of something different. But the details are fuzzy and fleeting. And it's just too exhausting to try. So, he doesn't usually try.

Darian is hated by everyone in his village and the surrounding countryside, with good reason. Whenever he's able to free himself from his bonds, the soldiers invariably find him, catch him, and chain him up again in this horrible place full of dead men's bones; this unclean place where the dead still walk, and dark spirits torture him. His captors throw scraps of food from a safe distance. Darian lunges and struggles against his chains when they come into sight, and he loves the way they jump, startled, suddenly afraid. Throw the food and run. He screams obscenities and laughs at them, cursing them for their cowardice.

And the chains. Darian is always able to break free of them, eventually. They haven't found any yet that will hold him for long. He compartmentalizes the pain, refusing to feel it as he strains against them. What will he do when he breaks these new ones? Steal some food first off. Lots of it. And God help anyone who gets in his way.

Something interrupts his reverie, jerking him back to the present. He strains again with all his strength, suddenly feeling his chains break apart. Freedom!

He hears something. What is that sound? Voices. But these are new ones Darian hasn't heard before. Some new game, maybe?

As the small group of men walk into sight, Darian, now free, lumbers toward them. He loves to smell their fear when he looms up in front of his unsuspecting victims. They're usually too terrified to run, so remain rooted to the ground, mouths agape, waiting; waiting to see what he might do to them.

But not this time.

Who is that man in the front? His calm stance clearly identifies him as the leader. All eyes in the group turn to him. Darian senses real authority emanating from this man. He can almost see it. What is he saying?

"What is your name?"

Suddenly Darian is on his knees, as an unseen hand forcefully throws him down and he hears his own voice, sounding strangely guttural in his ears, replying, "My name is Legion, for we are many." (Mark 5:9)

Eyes suddenly open wide and jaws drop. A nervous murmur spreads through the men gathered around their leader.

And then everything happens at once. That voice again – issuing a command that cannot be disobeyed.

Darian watches, as if from a distance, his own body contorting violently from a seizure. He falls heavily to the ground, roiling the dust at his feet, and at the same time he catches the unmistakable sound and smell of a herd of pigs running hard, as if from an unseen specter. He watches mesmerized, as they run, unheeding, straight off a cliff, plunging to their deaths in the water far below.

Darian's eyes close and a heavy sigh escapes his lips. And then his mind goes empty.

The next thing he knows, he's sitting on the ground fully clothed, and that man – someone called Him Jesus - is smiling at him. What happened?

Jesus speaks to Darian in a gentle voice filled with compassion and yes, there is, unmistakably, love in His eyes. Darian suddenly feels himself smiling back. And there is a joy bubbling in his heart he can't remember ever feeling before.

The conversation ended too soon for Darian's liking. He wanted more.

"Please, Rabbi, let me go with you. Let me follow along with you."

But Jesus tells him no. "I want you to go tell everyone in your village what wonderful things God has done for you."

Delivered. Released. Forgiven. Darian knows he'll spend the rest of his life finding the right words.

He owes Jesus so much.

This story, of all the stories about Jesus and His miracles, always made me wonder this

- why did He take the time to cross the lake to help this one man? A wicked and violent man.

In a word, Jesus saw value in him.

He waded right into the middle of Darian's mess, pain, and evil heart and changed him, loved him. As unlovable as Darian was, Jesus loved him anyway.

No one had asked Jesus to come and fix their Darian problem. There was no emissary sent out to beg for Jesus's help.

Jesus came anyway.

Why? What did Jesus see in Darian that was invisible to everyone else?

Jesus saw what Darian could be. He saw value where everyone else saw a throw-away and a problem- maker. And that's what he acted on. And that's what Darian responded to.

Value. Seeing value in others is another way to love.

The homeless person on the street corner. The convict, lonely in prison. The co-worker with different beliefs.

No matter where you are. No matter what you've done. It doesn't matter.

We too need to see the value that God sees.

We know what Jesus would do – because He already did it.

One day at the visiting camp, as they call the cinder block building with cafeteria-style tables, a couple of vending machines, and a small "canteen" where you can purchase over-priced food to heat up in a microwave, I met a young man about my son's age who was working the canteen. He was highly intelligent with the most beautiful and intense green eyes I've ever seen, respectful, and was in prison for a similar offense as my son's.

When he could, he'd spend a few minutes chatting with us and we all became friends. He was being transferred, so I asked him if I could write him and be his adoptive mom. He had little support and was estranged from his biological mom. He readily agreed.

And a correspondence began.

My main purpose in writing to Storm (yes, that's his first name – interesting, isn't it?) was to point him to Jesus. I wanted him to know he was valuable, and that Jesus died for him too.

Here's an excerpt from one of my letters:

I just recently finished reading, again, the book of Hebrews. I love that book! We aren't sure who wrote it, but the logic is irrefutable, and the subject matter is deep. I particularly like the part where the author speaks about how the law of Moses couldn't make anyone righteous, so a new priest, not one of the Levites but of the tribe of Judah, had to come and bring a new law. "What is old and obsolete is disappearing." Jesus brought the New Covenant where He wrote His law in our hearts and on our minds.

When I spend time with the believers at Northstar, I experience this — where each of us are invisibly linked to the other with this law that fills our minds and hearts with love for the one who sacrificed Himself for us. We are filled with joy when we serve each other and help to bring in the lost sheep.

For many years, my motto, if you will, has been this – one day I want to hear these words from my Savior: Well done, good, and faithful servant.

My prayer is that you will grow in knowledge and grace as you experience personally how very deeply God loves you.

Because I'm not an outgoing person, discouragement follows me around when I attempt to share important truths. But then I remember the Apostle Paul's encouraging words. We plant and God gives the increase. Now, I'm able to communicate the gospel with others as God lays it on my heart, knowing that He will do what is needed and perform the heart-miracles, no matter how well or poorly I've said or written what I've said or written.

Nice, right? If I can be used, so can you. Go find someone to mentor and encourage. You'll never be the same, and neither will they.

Storm wrote something very sweet in a Mother's Day card recently:

"Mom,

There's an old adage, "You can pick your friends but not your family." Because of you, I know that's not true.

> *I'm so grateful you decided to write me all those years ago.*
>
> *Thanks so much for being there, for everything.*
>
> *Love,*
> *Storm"*

There truly is no greater joy than knowing your children walk in the truth and that you were able to play a small part in their journeys.

Chapter 9

LET ME HELP YOU

She vowed it would never happen again. Yeah. A promise is a promise, she told herself. Good luck with that.

Time, as she knew, would soften the pain until it all but disappeared. That's what everyone always says. That's what all the books say.

Until then, though, she knew she needed to keep moving forward. Pain was part of growth, so let's get on with it.

She moved to this small, cozy town to get on with her life, but in a safe place. Adding personal touches made her small apartment finally feel like home. Watching the early morning sky unfold while sitting on her balcony, sipping that first cup of coffee, was heaven.

Peaceful and quiet.

Vanessa, a lover of color, had chosen cheery shades for the walls, each room glowing with a different palette: a restful blue for the living room, cheery yellow for the miniature kitchen and dining area, two shades of green for her bedroom, and a vibrant orange for her very own library. She lovingly placed her best friends – her well-read books – on the brand-new shelves. The dark wood was striking against the bright orange walls. And Vanessa thought her own personal library was the most inviting room ever. She could get lost, maybe for days, in one of her favorite stories, far away from her everyday life.

Speaking of moving forward, where was that letter? Her grandma wasn't going to learn how to use a computer – not in her lifetime, she always said – so her correspondence was longhand. Vanessa knew as soon as she saw the wobbly, spidery cursive, the letter would dredge up painful memories. So, she waited until evening to open it. She didn't want any distractions. There was solace in solitude.

Feet curled up under her, and with her favorite pillow – the one she'd found at the thrift store just down the street — tucked behind her, she gently opened the envelope, her hands trembling slightly, a faint scent of her grandma's perfume escaping. Vanessa sighed deeply, momentarily closing her eyes, pausing before focusing on the words she knew would bring her pain once again.

Growing up, she knew her life was different from her friends' lives. She wasn't quite sure why. There were those looks; the whispers that ceased when she entered a room. Maybe that's why she'd always been told she was painfully shy.

"You know what," she said to herself, "I'll tackle Grandma's letter tomorrow. Surely her message will keep until then." Her past was one book she wished would remain closed, like one of her old diaries from a lifetime ago – locked and hidden.

A Facebook friend recently posted a meme about procrastination. Yeah. How did it go? "Don't put off until tomorrow what you can pretend never happened at all."

It was tempting. Very tempting. She could shove the letter amidst the other undesirable things in her life drawer; her junk drawer. We all have them. At least one drawer in our houses for those miscellaneous things and prefer-to-have-out-of-sight things. We say to ourselves – "I'll deal with that next week." But we all know next week never actually gets here.

Until it slaps us in the face repeatedly, refusing to be ignored anymore.

Vanessa placed the letter on her side table, its whiteness shining like a beacon, and got up from her comfy chair. She absently picked up her glass of wine and took a sip, then another, and began pacing. And as she paced, she began to talk. Out loud. To him. Her carefully concealed anger surfaced and as she remonstrated, her pace quickened, her eyes growing bright with emotion. Her hands made slashing gestures in the air, and tears coursed down her face. The screaming seemed to come from a distant place of darkness where only fear lived.

She stopped in mid-tirade, face red and blotchy, her breath ragged, her body trembling; right in the middle of one of her favorite accusations. She had honed her arguments until they were as sharp as a cactus spike, but more deadly. Vanessa had practiced for years. She had it down pat. Her lines were memorized, and her gestures were carefully choreographed.

That very soft voice was here whispering in her ear. "Do you trust me?" She choked on a sob.

The voice that wouldn't leave her alone. It had followed her here, even here.

Vanessa, her face streaked with hot tears, looked around as if she would be able to see the presence behind the voice. She stood still and willed her breathing to slow. She was suddenly exhausted. Then she heard the voice once more, almost caressing in its softness. "Do you trust me?"

She knew who it was of course.

She sank to the floor and put her head in her hands.

Have you ever tried to help someone who wasn't ready to be helped? Your carefully chosen words, your exuberance, your expectation of acceptance, instantly shatters like shards of glass at your feet as your friend loses it emotionally and storms off.

Fractured people aren't broken dishes to be glued back together. A lot of time and effort, pain and heartache, are usually needed before any change will occur. Months, years, even decades, pass.

I have a friend who moved a few years back, leaving some of her belongings in a storage unit. Since she didn't have enough room yet at her new place, she put more personal items in another storage unit. Then, because of circumstances, some of her things are now stored in a friend's extra room, and her car is packed full of more things she totes around with her wherever she goes. Her "baggage," as you might put it, is scattered over a wide area.

It's hard to let go of the baggage of our lives, especially the most difficult parts, since they made the deepest impression on our minds and are scored most deeply into our hearts.

I can (and have) reasoned with my friend. "After paying storage fees for the past several years," I've said, "there's no monetary value left on any of your stuff. Maybe it's time to sell it or give it away and save your money for a security deposit on a nicer place." But my words are as ineffectual as a dull knife. Instead of cutting neatly and precisely, it only flattens and destroys, hurting our relationship.

I can clearly see what she needs to do, but that's only what I see. She sees things, or I should say feels things, differently. All that stuff – furniture, photos, memorabilia, tie her to her past and she's not ready to release it yet. Even though the past is painful and brings her little joy, those events have shaped who she is, for good or ill. They comprise much of her current identity. And the memory of those events is the baggage she stores, visits, and carts around.

It takes time to establish a new identity; an identity that is founded on a solid foundation. It takes time to release the past and build a new person, a person strong enough to look back occasionally, keeping the past where it belongs; in the past, and only moving forward with the lessons learned.

It takes a strong and resolute friend to hang in there, doing what needs to be done when it needs doing. It's hard to know sometimes just what that thing is.

We need to speak truth and faith into lives, making the crooked places smooth so the lame won't stumble.

Vanessa's eyes were leaking. She kept blinking back the tears so she could read what her grandma had written.

"I hope this letter finds you in health and safety, my dear child. I know in the past, my writing has only brought you pain, so I won't do it again. Never again.

I thought for years that I only had to explain the circumstances to you to make it all better, but I know now that I was lying to not just you but myself as well.

So, this letter is to tell you that I love you so very much! You are a wonderful, smart, beautiful woman and I couldn't be prouder of the person you've become. Your heart for others humbles me. Know I'm cheering you on from the sidelines.

Do you remember our song? The one I used to sing to you when you were a tiny, little thing? It was from Tarzan – You'll Be In My Heart by Phil Collins. We used to watch it together, remember?

'Come stop your crying
It will be alright
Just take my hand
And hold it tight

I will protect you
From all around you
I will be here
Don't you cry…

I'll never forget the first time I held you in my arms and looked deep into your eyes, your mother's eyes, and vowed to never let anything hurt you. I'm so sorry! I failed you miserably!

Please forgive an old woman, if you can find it in your heart. When you're ready, let me know how you're doing. Maybe someday we can be close friends once again.

All my love forever,
Grandma

Healing is a mystery of science. The body repairs its broken parts, leaving small scars as reminders. Healing hearts is a job for heroes.

"Having purified your souls by your obedience to the truth for a sincere brotherly love, love one another earnestly from a pure heart." (I Peter 1:22, ESV)

The word 'earnestly' is from the Greek – *ektenos*, meaning earnest, resolute, tense. It has the connotation of "stretching out." Going all in with your love; giving it everything you have with all the strength you have. Sounds like unconditional love to me.

Our friends need us to hang in there with them and never give up. Eternity is on the line.

Chapter 10

STORY PEOPLE

I mentioned earlier that I write articles for the local newspaper and a quarterly Christian magazine. To write the articles, I conduct interviews, both face to face and on the phone, depending on the circumstances.

I clearly remember sitting at a kitchen table with a cup of coffee, as two special mothers whose love for their children leaked out of their eyes. I was covering the terrible drug addiction problem we have in our local area, wanting to shed light on the collateral damage affected by this plague of horrific proportions. Patti's daughter was still struggling on and off with drug addiction, and she wasn't sure where her daughter even was at that time. Her son was finally on the right track after a year and a half in rehab, and her heart was broken because she had lost custody of her tiny granddaughter. Carol's story was heart-wrenching because her precious son had died of an overdose. He was gone, and she'd never hold him in her arms again or hear his laughter or see his smile. And she knew who the young man was who had given her son the drugs that killed him. He was alive, still dealing drugs and her baby was dead. We sat together and cried.

Another interview I did was with a friend who is in the process of adopting two young brothers who were delivered from terrible, abusive conditions; small children who should have never had to experience what they've endured in their short lives. Is this family wealthy? No. Do they have a big house and plenty of resources? No. She, her husband, and three teenaged children have what is more important. They have hearts big enough to love and adopt children with whom they are not related by blood. The pain and mess of these two young boys is now theirs. And they embrace it with joy.

Then there's the grandparents raising their curly-haired granddaughter because her momma died suddenly, unable to properly grieve their loss because of a new responsibility thrust upon them. Pouring themselves into this precious life for several years, only to make the gut-wrenching decision to let another family member adopt her, their home is now empty. Empty of their daughter's laughter and their granddaughter's presence, the grieving seems to never end.

I've interviewed men and women, hard-working and generous, who spend themselves in rescue missions, halfway houses, transitional housing, drug rehabilitation programs, and so much more to help the broken recover. They live with disappointment every day. And they still encourage the hurting every single day. They rejoice when an addict stays clean for a year. They mourn when they relapse. They absorb the anger and harsh words and temper tantrums, believing a better day is coming, believing in healing.

Then there are the Hurricane Michael survivors who spend themselves finding ways to help those who have even less than they have been left with. Homes destroyed. Personal possessions gone. Needing food and clothing, shelter and work. They hand out the little they have to someone else in greater need.

The hospice workers who bring comfort to families and hope to the dying: They answer those tough phone calls at all hours, knowing the news is never good news. They listen to the dying as they tell their own life stories, holding frail hands and gazing with love into failing eyes and stilling hearts. Their work not finished, they comfort the family and friends left behind. They have supernatural strength, but still mourn the loss of their new friends, already gone.

All these special people are my "story people." I have a bond with them now. We've shared our hearts and I've learned to appreciate all of these "regular folk" walking among us like angels who don't hold back when the going gets tough, but step right into someone else's pain, hurt, and need. They don't think about their own feelings but focus on what this other person – this valuable person – needs.

That, my readers, is what love is about. Love compels us to serve and heal. We can't sit on the sidelines anymore as spectators when we love.

The moment your spirit touches another spirit, an eternal bond is formed; a bond that cannot be ignored. I believe in order to be whole ourselves, we have to share pieces of ourselves with others. The wind, invisibly swirling around and through every living thing, gently hands us small shards of another soul, and only when they're placed together do they make us complete.

God has shown me what unconditional love is. May we all learn to practice it daily.

Epilogue

I had this fantastic idea for a book. I began writing, got stuck, put it away for some months, picked it back up, got stuck again, then put it away again.

That's when God showed me it wasn't time for that book. It was time for a different book.

I've been writing on and off for years, posting on blogs, writing articles for newspapers and magazines, conducting interviews, and saving other documents on my computer in various folders because I keep everything I write. This book, *Through Cracked Glass,* has been a compilation of many of those writings, along with new content to fill in the gaps which will, hopefully, make for smoother reading.

As I prayed over this book and its stories, I found some saved documents on my computer I hadn't remembered writing. It was astounding to me how so much of those previous writings fit in perfectly now. It's been an interesting, eye-opening journey putting this memoir together, encouraging me all over again. God's timing is perfect. He knew, when I wrote those short missives while going through storms in my life, that one day they would have a purpose and I'd find them at the right time to share with you.

For example, the introduction poem "Wings" for Section three on Serving was written in two parts years apart. The first half was written when I was doing some deep soul-searching in 2011. The second half came about several years later, around 2014, after I discovered that sometimes we're misunderstood in our mission, but we must keep on doing what God has called us to do, no matter what.

The vision about the young girl dancing in the meadow was written when I desperately needed some vindication about the mess my life seemed to be at the time. It was only a short little piece, but its imagery portrayed what I was feeling and the healing that God had begun in my heart.

The opening "Jess and the Sparrow" for the Forgiveness section came about some years

EPILOGUE

back while co-caregiving for my mom, and the struggles and pain that surfaced during that time. I know now that one of the reasons God put in my heart to serve my parents in the way I did was because of the baggage I had been dragging around, hindering me in my growth. I needed to finally and permanently lay it down at the foot of the cross. I was able to say good-bye to a lot of ghosts from my past and make peace with childhood pain. It cleared the air for both me and my mom, at least for the short time she still remembered that I was her daughter.

When I think back to my first blog, started almost ten years ago, it's amazing to re-read some of those posts that God had placed on my heart back when I just needed a place to share what I was learning; a place where I could put in writing what was happening to me, so I didn't feel alone anymore.

As frail and messed-up humans, we need to know we aren't alone in our struggles and pain. Community is important to our mental and spiritual health, so I pray that this book has helped you see that you are never alone.

There's a host of battle-scarred veterans of our own private wars willing to reach out our hands and help you up.

This may be the end of this memoir, but it's not the end of the life lessons God continues to teach me.

Who knows? Maybe I'll have to write a sequel in a decade or so.

Keep learning, keep growing, and hold fast to what you have.

It's all for Jesus.
Victoria

Bibliography

Evans, Richard Paul. *The Walk*. New York: Simon & Schuster, 2010.

Goff, Bob. *Everybody, Always*. Tennessee: Nelson Books, 2018.

Graham, Franklin. *Rebel With a Cause*. Tennessee: Thomas Nelson, Inc., 1995.

Idleman, Kyle. *Don't Give Up*. Michigan: Baker Books, 2019.

Lucado, Max. *Outlive Your Life*. Tennessee: Thomas Nelson, 2010.

Manning, Brennan. *The Furious Longing of God*. Colorado: David C. Cook, 2009.

Manning, Brennan. *The Ragamuffin Gospel*. Colorado: Multnomah Books, 2005.

Miller, Donald. *A Million Miles in a Thousand Years*. Tennessee: Thomas Nelson, 2009.

Sande, Kenneth. *The Peacemaker*. Michigan: Baker Books, 1991.

Spurgeon, C. "Psalm 63 by C. H. Spurgeon." Blue Letter Bible. Last Modified 5 Dec 2016. https://www.blueletterbible.org/Comm/spurgeon_charles/tod/ps063.cfm

Van Der Post, Laurens. *A Story Like the Wind*. New York: William Morrow and Company, 1972.

Wikipedia. "Jesus Loves Me", last accessed October 3, 2019. https://en.wikipedia.org/wiki/Jesus_Loves_Me

About the Author

Victoria is a feature writer for two local newspapers, *The Lynn Haven Ledger/Gulf Coast Gazette* and *Destin Life/SoWal Life*. She also writes and edits for the quarterly magazine *GO! Christian Magazine.*

She maintains a personal blog at *astoryinthewind.com,* where she showcases some of her published articles, stories, musings, the occasional writing lesson, and her day-to-day Arizona vacation experiences from April 2019.

Victoria is a mother and grandmother of not just biological children and grandchildren, but any and all ragamuffins who come across her path, since she recognizes her own ragamuffin-ness and need to be part of a family, too.

A native Michigander, then a temporary resident of Arizona, she currently lives in the Panhandle of Florida in Panama City Beach, within walking distance of the gorgeous Gulf of Mexico and its sugar-white sand and emerald waters.

She is thankful to have escaped the long, gray winters and bone-chilling cold of Michigan for the heat and sun of Florida, although she would prefer the low humidity, mountains, and desert of her beloved Arizona if she had her druthers.